# BABY BOEINGS

# BABY BOEINGS

ROBBIE SHAW

## ACKNOWLEDGEMENTS

Unfortunately the section of the book pertaining to the Next Generation 737 is not as complete as I would have liked it to be. This is due to a lack of co-operation from Boeing's PR department, who refused every request I made – quite a contrast from their counterparts at rival Airbus Industrie. I have since been told by a contact at Boeing that the refusal of access is due to me being a 'European' - such is Boeing's paranoia concerning Airbus!

On a more positive note, I would like to thank my wife Eileen for putting up with my absence, whether it be hidden in the study behind a word processor or sorting out slides, or in some far flung corner of the world with a heavy camera bag slung over my shoulder. She is also due credit for the somewhat tedious task of proof reading my efforts.

Robbie Shaw
*August 1998*

## EDITOR'S NOTE

To make the Osprey Civil Aircraft series as authoritative as possible, the editor would be interested in hearing from any individual who may have relevant information relating to the aircraft/operators featured in this, or any other, volume published by Osprey Aviation. Similarly, comments on the editorial content of this book would also be most welcome. Please write to Tony Holmes at 10 Prospect Road, Sevenoaks, Kent, TN13 3UA, Great Britain.

Published by Osprey Publishing, Michelin House,
81 Fulham Road, London SW3 6RB

© 1998 Osprey Publishing Limited

ISBN 1 85532 750 3

Edited by Tony Holmes
Page design by Paul Kime
Cutaway on pages 126/127 by Mike Badrocke

For a catalogue of all Aviation titles published by Osprey, please write to the Marketing Department, Osprey Publishing, 1st Floor, Michelin House, 81 Fulham Road, London SW3 6RB

Printed in Hong Kong

**FRONT COVER**
*Distinctively marked in the airline's traditional sky blue scheme, a Maersk Air 737-300 climbs out of Gatwick bound for Billund*

**BACK COVER**
*Amongst the rarest 727s to be captured on film are those of MIAT Mongolian Airlines – the letters MIAT stand for Mongolyn Irgeniy Agaaryn Teever. The airline has three former ANA and Korean Air 727-281s, the first of which arrived in July 1992. These 727s are seldom seen outside of the Chinese and Russian destinations they serve. MT-1054 was photographed taxying onto the runway at Beijing's Capital airport in March 1997*

**TITLE PAGE**
*LOT Polish Airlines began services from Gatwick to Krakow in 1997, and in 1998 will inaugurate a Gdansk service. 737-500s like SP-LKF, seen here climbing out of the London airport, operate most flights*

**OPPOSITE**
*A 737-200 of British Airways is seen about to land at its Gatwick base. The -200s are approaching the end of their long careers with 'BA', forcing the airline to hastily look for a replacement*

# Contents

**LEFT** *To promote the launch of its new Stansted-Prestwick service in late 1995,
Ryanair adorned EI-CJD with a tartan scarf around the forward fuselage just behind
the cockpit. The image was completed with a smile painted on the nose cone*

# Introduction

*Baby Boeings* contains photographic coverage of the two most successful jet airliners ever built – namely the 727 and 737. As if to reinforce this point, by the time these words are read, Boeing will have delivered its 3000th 737! Whilst these aircraft can hardly be described as 'babies', other models from the same stable – notably the 747 and 777 – are truly leviathans by comparison.

## BOEING 727

With the commercial introduction of the de Havilland Comet in 1952, it soon became apparent that jet power was the way forward for future airliners. Boeing's answer to the British design was the 707 and slightly smaller 720, and although these aircraft were more than capable of performing the medium- to long-haul routes across both America and the globe, a number of major US carriers also expressed a need for a short-range jet-powered aircraft too. As a result of these requests, Boeing began studies into what would eventually become the 727 in 1957. A number of potential designs and layouts were looked at, ranging from a four-engined 'baby 707' to two- and three-engined designs. The majority of potential US customers wanted an aircraft with good field performance and easy maintenance for quick turn-rounds, the latter aspect of the request rapidly ruling out the four-engined 'baby 707' idea.

As the tri-jet proposals did not meet with enthusiasm, the twin-engined design seemed the obvious choice. However, at that time the paucity of suitably powerful engines effectively stopped the 'twin' jet airliner in its tracks, Pratt & Whitney, for

**LEFT** *First customer for the 727 series 200 was Northwest Orient Airlines. Now known simply as Northwest, the operator currently flies 42 727-200Adv aircraft such as N289US, which is now in its 20th year of service with the airline, and is seen here about to land at Detroit in May 1991*

**BELOW LEFT** *American Airlines (whose fleet at one time included over 100 examples of the Boeing tri-jet) was an early customer for the 727. The venerable airliner still plays a major part in the operator's route network, with 79 -200s remaining in use into the final quarter of 1997. Illustrated taxying for departure at Buffalo in June 1992 is series 100 N1991. This aircraft was delivered to American in 1965 but was disposed of in 1994. It has since been converted into a freighter and operates in South Africa – see chapter one*

RIGHT *United Airlines was the launch customer for the 737 series 200 with an order for 40 aircraft, the first example of which was delivered just a few days after Lufthansa received its first series 100. United ultimately operated over 70 -200s, and by the end of 1997 still had 64 of the type in its inventory. United has, however, already found buyers for a number of these aircraft, which are about to be replaced by Airbus A319s. Photographed in the airline's old colours at Cleveland, Ohio, in 1995 is 737-222 N9017U, which has the distinction of being only the 37th 737 built. It is still in use today*

example, showing little interest in spending money on developing such a powerplant. With no prospect of purchasing a suitable engine in America, Boeing looked eastward across the Atlantic to Rolls-Royce, whose Spey engine project revealed a powerplant eminently suitable for the company's new product.

Just when Boeing thought they had at last found an answer to their 'thrust' problem, some of the airliner's potential customers made it clear they would not accept an aircraft powered by foreign engines, so it was back to the drawing board for the design team. Sadly, the 'NIH' ('Not Invented Here') attitude is still prevalent in some areas of the US aviation/airline industry today. Ultimately, Boeing's interest in the Rolls-Royce engine was the spur needed for Pratt & Whitney to get its act together, and they eventually produced the JT8D-1 engine specifically for the 727.

Whilst looking at possible configurations, Boeing undertook research into delays at New York airports, and came up with some interesting results. When flights into New York were subjected to bad weather, the FAA (Federal Aviation Administration) imposed more severe safety limitations on twin-engined aircraft than they did on four-engined types. The latter were permitted a decision height of 200 ft, whilst the former observed a ceiling of 300 ft. The 100 ft difference between the two heights had a crucial effect on the number of twin-engined types suffering from flight curtailment due to adverse weather conditions. During discussions with the FAA, it transpired that a tri-jet would be permitted to operate to the 200 ft decision height. This was

a major factor in deciding on a tri-jet layout, particularly as when pressed, the majority of potential customers had no major objection to such a layout.

Back across the Atlantic in Britain, de Havilland were proceeding with the DH 121 Trident, a tri-jet designed specifically for BEA (British European Airways). de Havilland visited Seattle at an early stage in the aircraft's development, and serious discussions took place on Boeing producing the Trident under licence for the

North American market. However, despite the US manufacturer being very interested in de Havilland's proposals, in certain areas the Trident was not compatible with the design requested by American domestic operators. Potential customers for the Boeing model specified a take-off run of some 5000 ft to enable it to operate from the many regional airports with runways of about that length. In contrast, the Trident required a take-off run of some 6000 ft, as BEA would be flying the type into major European airports with long runways. Over the years BEA continually chopped and changed its requirements for the Trident, and the airline can take most of the blame for ruining the long term prospects of a potentially good aircraft – the Trident's reluctance to get airborne in less than 6000 ft earned it the nickname 'Gripper' from its crews!

The tri-jet proposal was given the go-ahead in June 1959, with formal launch of the 727 announced at a press conference

*Britannia Airways was the first European airline to put the 737-200 into service in 1968, which was quite an amazing feat for a charter airline. The 737 served Britannia well, and at one time it had as many as 29 on strength, including former Orion Airways series -300s. Britannia's fleet now comprises 757s and 767s, although four A320s are to be leased for the 1998 summer season. Seen taxying for departure at Glasgow in 1988 is 737-204 G-BKHF Sir Alliot Verdon Roe. This aircraft currently serves with Ryanair as EI-CJF*

on 5 December 1960. The new airliner would feature a fuselage with the same width as the 707 and 720 – a feature which has since been repeated with the 737 and 757, and which is a major selling point that has proven popular with customers. The 'T-tailed' tri-jet would be powered by three Pratt & Whitney JT8D-1 engines each rated at 14,000 lb thrust. Passenger capacity ranged from around 90 in a two-class configuration up to 125 in high density all-economy. The 727 was the first Boeing jet airliner with full powered flight controls (hydraulically-powered dual units being fitted), the one exception to this system being the electrically-trimmed horizontal stabiliser. It was also the first aircraft to feature triple-slotted trailing edge flaps which, combined with the leading edge slats, give the 727 an exceptional take-off and landing performance.

The prototype was rolled out at Boeing's Renton plant in the Seattle suburbs on 27 November 1962, and took to the

air on its maiden flight on 9 February 1963 – 13 months after the first flight of the Trident. Initial deliveries were to launch customers United and Eastern, and it was the latter who operated the first service on 1 February 1964 – 39 days ahead of the Trident. Over the next few years a total of 408 standard 727-100s (including the prototype) were built. Added to this figure were 164 727-100C aircraft, this variant having been announced in August 1964. The suffix 'C' stood for convertible, the aircraft featuring a large cargo door in the port forward fuselage, which allowed the -100C to be used either in passenger, cargo or Combi configuration.

Always astute at commercially exploiting a sound design, Boeing quickly realised the growth potential of the 727. In August 1965 (by which time some 170 aircraft had been delivered) the company unveiled the 'stretched' series 200, which could carry up to 189 passengers and enjoyed a significant increase in range. The proto-type (the 433rd 727 built) flew on 27 July 1967 and the first production example entered service with Northwest Orient five months later. Concurrent with Boeing's airframe development, Pratt & Whitney continued to develop more powerful variants of the JT8D engine – the ultimate JT8D variant fitted to the 727 was the -17R, rated at 17,400 lb.

The final 727s built were the specialised -200F freighters, 15 being delivered to Federal Express in the early 1980s. The last of these was the 1260th 727-200 constructed by Boeing, and its delivery to FedEx on 18 September 1984 marked the end of a production run that had been sustained for more than 20 years, during which time 1832 727s had been built. This final figure made the 727 easily the best-selling airliner of all time up to that point, which was no mean achievement for an aircraft which, in the programme's infancy, had been expected to realise sales of between 250 and 400 units according to Boeing's marketing and sales division. The same people would get their figures wrong yet again, only on a much grander scale, with the 727's little brother, the 737.

## BOEING 737

Even while the 727 was preparing for its maiden flight, Boeing was already looking at the possibility of producing a smaller, cheaper, and even more cost effective short-range jet. In view of the initial reluctance of some members of the Boeing board of directors to sanction the 727 programme, this was a surprising move indeed. However, the initial batch of early orders for the tri-jet may have dispelled any doubts as to the success of the new model, designated the 737. Formally launched on 19 February 1965, the 737 assumed the mantle of the world's most successful airliner from the 727 exactly 25 years to the day from when it was announced with the delivery of the 1833rd aircraft.

With the 737, Boeing reverted to engines underslung in pods beneath the wing, the powerplant chosen for the aircraft being the JT8D-1, which had been fitted to the first 727s. The manufacturer also reverted to a more conventional tail unit, while for commonality, the fuselage width was identical to the Boeing tri-jet. The initial 737 variant was designated the series 100, and was capable of carrying 100 passengers in a mixed configuration cabin.

With major US carriers in the process of taking delivery of their first batches of 727s just as the 737 was announced, it probably came as no great surprise to Boeing that customers proved to be somewhat reluctant to part with further cash and invest in the smaller jetliner. After all, at that time the 727 was also exclusively a short-range jet – it was only later in its career that it evolved into a medium range transport.

With US airlines proving unimpressed with the new Boeing 'twin', it fell to German operator Lufthansa to act as launch customer for the 737. This was the first time a foreign airline had filled such a role, although Boeing products were not new to Lufthansa, for it had earlier become the first operator outside North America to select the 727, which had joined the 707 on the airline's route network.

Aside from meeting stiff resistance from

US airlines already committed to an earlier Boeing product, the 737 also faced a major domestic competitor in the shape of the Douglas DC-9, not to mention the British Aircraft Corporation's BAC One-Eleven in European markets.

The prototype 737 first flew on 9 April 1967, but only 30 series 100s were built before the arrival of the larger series 200. Announced by Boeing prior to the first flight of the prototype 737-100, the series 200 featured a slightly longer fuselage to accommodate up to 130 passengers and more powerful engines. It soon became the standard 737, with the variant's first flight from Renton taking place on 8 August 1967. United Airlines served as the launch customer, placing an initial order for 40 aircraft – as noted earlier, the airline had previously been a launch customer for the 727.

Although hard to believe now, 737 sales were very sluggish in the early days, and Boeing had concerns that it would not reach the break even target. However, sales steadily picked up with the advent of the -200, and the 737's development history during the 1970s mirrored that of the 727. The -200C and QC variants were introduced, followed by the -200 Advanced which, thanks to the use of graphite composites, reduced the weight of the airframe with a corresponding increase in maximum payload. Eventually the -200 proved to be a resounding success, with 1114 aircraft built – the final example was delivered to Xiamen Airlines in China in August 1988.

Buoyed by the ever-increasing sales of the 737-200, but aware that rival airliners from McDonnell Douglas and Airbus Industrie were starting to make their aircraft look rather old, Boeing's design teams worked hard to improve their product. The end result was the 'New Generation' series – the -300, -400 and -500. The major difference between the old -200 and the New Generation variants centres around the powerplant adopted by Boeing, namely the more powerful, and considerably quieter, General Electric CFM56-3 turbofan engine. The new 737s also feature a 'glass' cockpit chocked full of advanced avionics. All three models have a common wing span, which is slight wider than the -200, although the fuselage height and width remain the same as the earlier 737. The series 300 is 2.87 m (9 ft 5 in) longer than the -200, and can seat up to 149 passengers, whilst the -400 has been 'stretched' further still and can take as many as 170 in an all-economy fit. Despite the increased size of these variants, Boeing did not ignore the demand from airlines for an aircraft with the capacity of the earlier -200, and duly produced the -500.

The first -300 flew on 24 February 1984, and initial examples were delivered to Southwest Airlines and USAir. Piedmont Airlines was the launch customer for the -400, the prototype of which flew on 19 February 1988. The first -500 completed its maiden flight on 30 June 1989, with launch customers Southwest and Braathens taking early deliveries. The series -300 soon became a favourite, with 252 being ordered in 1985 alone – by December 1997 sales of the -300 had exceeded that of the -200, with 1122 ordered. Once again Lufthansa was a valued customer, taking delivery of all three New Generation variants. On 25 February 1991 the German airline received its 100th 737 which, coincidentally, was the 2000th built.

Despite the continued success of the 737 family, competition was increasingly forthcoming from Airbus Industrie with its excellent A320 family. More and more customers were being lost to the European consortium, and Boeing had to do something to stem the tide. After consultation with many valued customers, it became apparent that most wanted a variant of the 737 which could fly higher, faster, more economically and with an increased payload and range. To improve on a highly successful product is no mean feat, however Boeing's designers set to work, and on 17 November 1993 announced the launch of its Next Generation series, originally known as the 737X.

The new variants featured the same fuselage height and width as all previous models, but thanks to the manufacturer's experience with the 777, the cabin interior was improved to give a wide-bodied look. They also incorporated an increased wing span and taller fin into the 737X. The new wing meant an increase in wing area by some 25 per cent, which allowed a 30 per cent increase in fuel capacity. The engine selected was the more powerful CFM-56-7. Initially, three models of the Next Generation aircraft were launched – the -600, -700 and -800. The first to fly was the -700, which completed its maiden flight on 9 February 1997. Similar in size and capacity to the -300, the -700's launch customer is Southwest Airlines, who have ordered no less than 63 aircraft, with options for a further 63. Maersk Air was the first overseas customer, and it has since been joined by a number of other European operators.

Next type to appear from the Renton production line is the larger -800, which is

*11 February 1998 saw the 3000th 737 built (a series 400 for Alaska Airlines) preparing to depart a rather wet Renton on its maiden flight*

3.02 m (9 ft 11 in) longer than the series 400, and can carry up to 189 passengers in a high density fit. The smallest of the trio is the series 600, which is very similar in size and capacity to the -500. The -600 only performed its first flight on 22 January 1998, and although SAS was the launch customer for this variant, sales have been rather slow to accumulate. Despite this, orders for the Next Generation series have in the main been staggering, and by the time of the Paris Airshow in June 1997, an amazing 627 aircraft had been sold to 29 customers. This is a phenomenal figure considering that none had yet been delivered to a customer – indeed, only one of the variants (-700) had even flown up to that point.

Boeing has also developed a corporate version known as the Boeing Business Jet (BBJ), which is based on the -700, but features the strengthened wing and landing gear of the -800. This specialist variant has also attracted a sizeable order book.

With the Next Generation aircraft still very much in their development phase, it therefore came as something of a surprise when on 10 November 1997 Boeing announced yet another new variant – the series 900, which is even longer than the -800. Launch customer is Alaska Airlines, who have opted for ten.

Almost as surprising as the speed at which the new Boeing 'twin' has appeared is the fact that the manufacturer has launched this aircraft on the back of just a single order from one customer. No doubt there must be others close to signing a deal, which is undoubtedly aimed at competing against the A321. These Next Generation models will, for the first time, allow the 737 to operate coast to coast

US domestic sectors, transforming the aircraft into a truly medium range jet.

Towards the end of 1997 Boeing temporarily ceased production of the 737 and 747. This drastic measure was implemented ostensibly to give sub-contractors time to build up stocks of parts due to the increased production rate. Rumour has it, however, that the primary reason for the halt may have been because the FAA had expressed concern over quality assurance of both types leaving the factory, resulting in possible safety oversights. In the wake of the loss of the Silk Air 737-300 on 19

December 1997 it was found that a number of fasteners were missing from the leading edge of the horizontal stabiliser. Although this could have been caused by the forces exerted on the aircraft as it fell from altitude, the FAA was concerned enough to issue a directive to carry out inspections on 211 series 300, 400 and 500 aircraft, a small number of which were found to have missing or loose fasteners. It certainly does seem strange work practice that Boeing would dispense with the services of thousands of employees just when orders for its products were rolling in at almost record levels.

By 31 January 1998 total orders for all 737 variants numbered 3941, and the 3000th aircraft – a series 400 for Alaska Airlines – flew on 11 February 1998. The very first 737 has only recently been delivered to the Museum of Flight in Seattle, 30 years, 5 months and 12 days after its maiden flight. The aircraft had spent the past 26 years in service with NASA as N515NA at the Langley Research Center at Hampton, Virginia, where it had been designated the Transport Systems Research Vehicle (TSRV).

# CHAPTER 1
# Boeing 727-100

When Boeing launched the 727 it announced that the prototype would fly 15 months later – a very ambitious aim indeed. It was therefore a considerable achievement when, under the command of Len Wallick, N7001U took to the air on 9 February 1963, beating the company deadline by a month.

It later transpired that just after rotation the centre engine experienced a momentary surge. This happened several times during testing until a change to the internal profile of the engine intake helped eradicate the problem. Although destined for United Airlines, the first aircraft initially faced many months of flight testing and certification work prior to delivery. The first ten hours of this work was carried out from Paine Field, Everett, now the site of 747, 767 and 777 production. The

**RIGHT** *A significant number of 727-100s are still in use, with many having been converted into cargo configuration. American International Airways (perhaps better known by its former name of Connie Kalitta) has a substantial fleet of freighter aircraft, including DC-8s, L-1011s and 747s, as well as 727s – both -100s and -200s. One of three -100s in the fleet, N727CK – a series -22C, whose previous owners include United and Air Canada – was captured on film about to touchdown at Buffalo, New York, in June 1995*

majority of the other test flights were conducted from Boeing Field, just a few miles away from Renton, although some flights were also originated from Edwards Air Force Base and Denver.

The second aircraft to fly was N72700 which flew on 12 March 1963. This 727 spent its entire life as a company demonstrator and test aircraft, whilst the third tri-jet (and second for United) took to the air on 10 April and also joined the test programme. So well was the test programme going that only six months after the prototype first flew, Boeing felt confident enough to send the fourth aircraft on a six-week long world sales and demonstration tour. This included visits to India, Pakistan, Thailand, the Philippines and Japan, before heading 'down under' to Australia. From there the return journey routed through Africa and Europe.

United and Eastern Airlines took delivery of their first aircraft in October and

ABOVE *727 freighters often ply their trade at night, when landing slots at major airports are easier to come by. One of those nocturnal tri-jets is Emery 727-44(F) N94GS, seen here resting between flights at Los Angeles alongside a company DC-8. This aircraft began its career in the passenger role with South African Airways in 1965*

**ABOVE** *Kelowna Flightcraft of Kelowna, British Columbia, is Canada's largest 727 operator with some 19 aircraft – a mix of -100s and -200s. Seven of the -100 freighters are operated in the colours of Purolator Courier, including 727-22C C-GFKZ, seen here during a daytime rest at Hamilton, Ontario. The large cargo door in the forward port fuselage is clearly visible*

November 1963, and immediately started training crews in anticipation of the FAA release to service, which came on 20 December 1963.

When Boeing announced the launch of the 727 it did so on the back of orders for 40 aircraft each for United and Eastern Airlines – two of the major US airlines the sales team had originally targeted. The third customer, and first overseas operator, was Lufthansa, who signed an order for 12 aircraft in March 1961. A further boost was received two months later when American Airlines signed a letter of intent for 25 727-100s. This airline would eventually become one of the largest operators of the type. Later, TWA (Trans World Airlines) joined the customer list, which came as something of a surprise as the airline had already signed an order for French-built SE 210 Caravelles powered by General Electric engines. To ease a growing cash flow problem, the airline

approached Boeing to ask for more time to pay for 707s it then had on order, and the outcome was that TWA got extended credit and Boeing an order for ten 727s. Not surprisingly, the Caravelle order was subsequently cancelled.

By the time of the initial roll out of the prototype 727, two further small, but nonetheless significant, orders had been announced, with Ansett and Trans Australian Airlines both buying a pair apiece. This took total orders to 131 from seven customers. The demonstration tour by production aircraft No 4 soon paid dividends too when both All Nippon Airways (ANA) and Japan Airlines ordered the 727. Both customers had initially looked like buying the rival Trident, whilst repeat orders were also received from Australia.

United Airlines was the first operator to receive an aircraft. Indeed the prototype N7001U, which was subsequently delivered to United at the cessation of its test flying programme, served with the airline until 13 January 1991 when it was donated to the Museum of Flight in Seattle. Despite getting aircraft first, United was beaten into second place in respect to introducing the type into fare-paying service by Eastern Airlines, who performed their first flight on 1 February 1964 from Miami to Washington and Philadelphia. By the end of 1963, Boeing was producing five aircraft a month, and within a year this figure had risen to eight.

The aircraft had barely been in service six months when in August 1964 Boeing announced an important new variant – the -100C. Capable of being configured for passengers, cargo or both, the -100C was soon dubbed the Combi. The variant featured a large outward and upward swinging door in the port forward fuselage and a strengthened cabin floor, with an integral conveyor system for cargo containers – some of the late-build Combis also had a strengthened centre fuselage and undercarriage.

Reconfiguration from one role to another took several hours, although this time scale was significantly reduced with the introduction of the QC (Quick Change) variant. This version had rows of seats and a galley mounted on the base of a pallet in order to ease installation, and thus quicken the conversion time – over half of the 164 -100C variants built were completed or retrofitted to QC standard. The first -100C (the 211th 727 built)

**TOP RIGHT** *To cope with the increasing noise restrictions being enforced at many airports in Europe and the USA, a number of 727s are being hushkitted or re-engined. United Parcel Service has decided on the latter option, even for its venerable fleet of -100s, the airline contracting the Dee Howard Company to refit 44 'short' 727 freighters with Rolls-Royce Tay 651 engines, as well as updating cockpit avionics with modern EFIS displays. Once converted, these aircraft are given the designation 727QF (Quiet Freighter), and are easily identifiable by the revised shape of the air intake of the number two engine — illustrated is 727-22C(QF) N930UP (photo by Tom Singfield)*

entered service with Northwest Orient Airlines on 13 April 1966.

The last 727-100 built — Line No 869 — was delivered to the ITT Corporation as N320HG in November 1971. Total production, including the prototype, numbered 408 standard -100s and 164 -100Cs, giving a total of 572 aircraft. Some 370 remain in use today, 300 of which are operated in the Americas — a number of these aircraft are over 30 years old. Although most of the world's major airlines have disposed of their 727s, the type is still in widespread use in the USA, whilst increasing numbers are appearing in both South America and Africa. The -100 is also a favourite in the corporate business jet sphere, while more and more ex-passenger aircraft are appearing as freighters on the civil register.

The major problem now facing elderly 727s centres on the jet's noisy and dirty JT8D-1 engines, which have been deemed unsuitable for use from many airports across the globe. Banned altogether from some noise sensitive European centres, the 727 is also restricted at other destinations, or barred from operating at night. To get around this problem, some operators are now looking at re-engining or hushkitting aircraft to meet stringent Stage 3/Chapter 3 noise limitations.

One such operator is airfreight giant Federal Express, who, rather than go to the expense of buying replacements for its large 727 fleet, are hushkitting its aircraft with Valsan conversion kits, which comprise acoustic nacelles on the outboard engines. United Parcel Service (UPS) has gone even further by contracting the Dee Howard Company to refit all 44 of its -100Cs with Rolls-Royce Tay 651

engines — these aircraft are known as 727QFs (Quiet Freighters), and are easily recognisable by the revised contours of the centre engine intake. The jets are also being equipped with a modern 'glass cockpit' at the same time. For the company to invest such a large sum of money in a fleet of 30-year-old aircraft is perhaps the ultimate tribute to the structural integrity of the 727, and should guarantee the sight of the distinctive Boeing tri-jet in American skies well into the next century.

**BELOW** *A number of 727-100s are in use as corporate executive jets, particularly in America. 727-21 N7271P is operated by Imperial Palace Inc, the VIP-appointed tri-jet having started its career in 1966 with Pan American as N320PA* Clipper Berlin

**RIGHT** *Following Latvia's independence from the former Soviet Union, the local Aeroflot division was renamed Latavio and designated the national carrier. In 1992 the independent airline Baltic International was also formed, initially with DC-9s, but later with a pair of former American Airlines 727-100s. In 1995, Baltic International and Latavio merged to form Air Baltic, which currently operates three Avro RJ70s. Photographed at London Gatwick in December 1994 is 727-23 YL-BAE City of Riga*

BELOW LEFT *Latin America and the Caribbean are home to many 727s operating with a variety of small, and not so small, airlines throughout the continent. Aero Costa Rica's inventory comprises a pair of 1964-vintage ex-American Airlines 727-23s, which were acquired in April 1996. Photographed preparing to depart Miami for San Jose, this aircraft is now in its 34th year of service, and has spent all of its life with the registration N1974*

BELOW, FAR LEFT *The bright yellow fuselage of this 727 immediately identifies it as an Itapemirim Cargo aircraft, the company operating four -100 and two -200 727 freighters. As one of the former, PP-ITA previously served with Cruzeiro, and is seen here taxying at its base, Rio de Janeiro's Galeao airport*

**BELOW LEFT** *Featured earlier in the introduction section of this book in American Airlines colours as N1991, this series 100 aircraft was photographed at Johannesburg's Jan Smuts airport in February 1996 whilst on a six-month lease to Zimbabwe Express Airlines as ZS-NMY. It has subsequently been converted into a freighter and remains in South Africa with Millionair Charter*

**BELOW RIGHT** *As a trial to measure potential fuel savings, Delta Airlines fitted winglets (not visible in this photograph) to two of its 727-200s, and Royal, in Canada, did likewise with one of its aircraft. Neither carrier opted to fit these devices to any of its other aircraft, however, and to my knowledge no other airline has followed suit. A small number of corporate 727 operators have undertaken such a conversion, including a company known as HMS Airways. This outfit operate two Jordanian-registered 727s (a -100 and a -200), both of which have winglets. Aircraft JY-HS1 is a 727-76 which was acquired in February 1996, and is seen at Heathrow in January 1998*

**ABOVE** Brussels based European Air Transport operates a fleet of Convair CV-580 and 727 freighter aircraft on behalf of, and in the colours of, DHL. The 727 fleet comprises 12 aircraft, divided evenly between -100s and -200s, and all are hushkitted to comply with Stage Three noise limitations. 727-35(F) OO-DHR was photographed at Gatwick on 24 August 1994

# CHAPTER 2
# Boeing 727-200

Although the 727-100 programme enjoyed excellent sales throughout the early to mid 1960s, and was well on the way towards the numbers predicted by the marketing team, Boeing soon found growth potential in the basic design.

In August 1965 (by which time some 170 aircraft had been delivered) Boeing announced the launch of the stretched series 200. This aircraft featured a 3.05 m (10 ft) plug both fore and aft of the wings, allowing for a significant increase in capacity to a maximum of 189 passengers. Powered by three JT8D-9 turbofans rated at 14,000 lb, this variant initially offered very little improvement in maximum take-off weight (MTOW) compared to the -100. However, the subsequent availability of the JT8D-9A rated at 14,500 lb and the -11 at 15,000 lb soon rectified this. The air intake for the centre engine was also revised, while the baggage hold doors

RIGHT *The fleet complement of American Trans Air has remained unchanged for several years, comprising 727s, 757s and L-1011 TriStars. Numerically, the 727 predominates, with 24 second-hand -200Adv aircraft currently in use. Featuring the airline's upbeat new livery on approach to Los Angeles is 727-214Adv N754US, this aircraft having initially been delivered new to Pacific Southwest Airlines, then acquired by Piedmont, who were in turn taken over by USAir*

were changed to open outwards rather then inwards.

The -200 proved very popular with major US carriers, many of whom ordered it in significant numbers to supplement their fleets of -100s. Before long, a number of European national carriers had also followed suit.

The prototype, registered N7270L, was the 433rd 727 built, and it first flew on 27 July 1967. Certification followed on 30 November, with the type entering service with Northeast Airlines in December 1967. Sales of the standard -200 were a little disappointing, however, with only 306 built.

It was due to the sluggishness of sales around 1969/70 that Boeing looked for a means to further improve the tri-jet, particularly with possible competition on the horizon from both McDonnell Douglas and Airbus Industrie. An improvement in the aircraft's range was deemed to be the best way to improve the 727, and thus make it into a truly medium range airliner. To achieve this, more powerful engines were fitted to enable the aircraft to cruise higher and more economically, plus carry a heavier payload over a greater distance. The Pratt & Whitney JT8D-15 rated at 15,500 lb was chosen for the job, the powerplant allowing the MTOW to be increased by some 22,000 lb to 191,000 lb. The new engines also permitted a staggering increase in range by up to 40 per cent.

Labelled the 727-200 Advanced, this variant was formally launched in December 1970 with an order from ANA.

Despite the increase in power from the new engine, Pratt & Whitney and Boeing successfully implemented modifications which enabled them to reduce the noise levels of the 727-200Adv to below that of any other commercial jet airliner then in service. The maiden flight of the first -200Adv (the 881st 727 built) was completed on the leap year day of 29 February 1972. The aircraft was eventually handed over to ANA as JA8343, and ultimately the -200Adv became so popular that it was built in greater numbers than any other 727 variant.

To cope with the heavier weight associated with this version, the centre section of the aircraft was strengthened and the landing gear featured larger tyres and improved brake units. A number of airlines which had already committed to the -200 converted their orders to the more powerful and popular version. This was particularly true in the Middle East, where Libyan Arab Airlines, Royal Air Maroc and TunisAir all took delivery of the advanced variant.

During a five-year period in the mid-1970s, over 100 aircraft were ordered each year, with production increasing to a maximum of 11.5 aircraft a month by 1980.

In February 1972 a further increase in

MTOW to 208,000 lb was announced thanks to the 16,000 lb-rated JT8D-17. Danish charter airline Sterling Airways was the first to order the 'heavyweight' version with the MTOW increased to 210,000 lb, thus allowing it to fly substantial sector routes such as Copenhagen-Tenerife and Copenhagen-Toronto. In November 1976 a yet more powerful variant was certified thanks to the fitment of the 17,400 lb-rated JT8D-17R engine. The latter also featured Automatic Performance Reserve (APR), which sensed any significant loss of thrust by an engine during take-off and automatically increased thrust on the other engines to compensate.

This engine combination was specifically designed for hot/high operations, making it ideal for Mexicana, who ordered a substantial number. A few have subsequently been sold to Qatar Airways, who use the type in the Arabian Gulf where temperatures in the summer can easily top 40°C. The last passenger 727 built was Line No 1817 destined for Iraqi Airways. However, due to political problems – the war with

**LEFT** *Continental Airlines is slowly modernising its fleet with new 757s and 737-500s, and with an ever-expanding intercontinental route network, the airline is also buying up second-hand DC-10s wherever it can find them. Its 42-strong 727 fleet is likely to soldier on for a few years yet, however, but they should eventually be replaced by new 737-800s. This shot of 727-224 N88704 in Continental's old livery at Newark dates back to 1990. Its sister-ship taxying behind it is interesting as it is still basically painted in the old People Express colour scheme, over which Continental's titling, cheatlines and tail logo have been applied*

**BELOW** *Delta Airlines currently has the largest fleet of 727 passenger jets, with only Fedex operating more examples of the Boeing tri-jet (of course its aircraft are freighter-configured). Delta's fleet of 727-200Adv currently numbers an amazing 129 aircraft, some of which were acquired in the take-over of Western Airlines. Seen on the taxyway at Phoenix on 26 March 1995 is 727-232Adv N489DA*

Iran was raging at the time – the aircraft was never delivered to its intended customer (who already operated several of the type), being subsequently delivered to USAir instead in March 1983.

The final 727 variant announced in October 1981 was the -200F freighter for Federal Express. Totally devoid of cabin windows, this variant was built to the tune of just 15 airframes all for FedEx. As the last 727s ever built, the delivery of Line No 1832 (registered N217FE) to FedEx on 18 September 1984 brought production to a close. Complementing these dedicated freighters, a number of ex-passenger -200s have now also been converted into cargo carriers.

A total of 1260 series 200s were built, and around 950 of these are still providing sterling service today. The combined total for all 727 variants is 1832 aircraft.

Like the -100, the -200 is still going strong particularly in the USA, and airlines such as American, Delta, Fedex and United all have fleets of around 100 aircraft –

indeed, Delta still has 131 727s in service. South American airlines also seem to be continually increasing the size of their 727 fleets, while conversely, operators in Europe are steadily shedding their Boeing tri-jets in order to comply with stringent noise restriction regulations that have been imposed at many European airports. With even stricter controls on noise and pollution emissions soon to come into force within the EEC, a number of airlines on the continent will have to take a serious look at either fitting hushkits to their aircraft, or replacing them altogether.

Many modern airliners now feature winglets which improve the aerodynamics

and assist in reducing fuel consumption. Following this trend, Delta Airlines fitted winglets to two of its 727 aircraft in 1993 as part of a trial to see if the possible fuel saving would justify modifying its entire fleet of tri-jets. After a number of months in service, the jets revealed no great reduction in their appetite for fuel, so the airline decided against the retrofit. However, prior to the results being made public, Canadian charter airline Royal also fitted winglets to one of its -200s. Some corporate 727 operators have also adapted their aircraft with winglets since the Delta Airlines trial, this modification being seen on both -100s and -200s. That an aircraft well into its third decade of service can still be valued highly enough to warrant expenditure on such cost-saving, and therefore life-extending, projects is a tribute to the 727's structural integrity and longevity.

Boeing had planned to upgrade the 727 and develop a series -300, featuring a further fuselage stretch and potential engine power provided by the Rolls-Royce RB.211, but in the end this development was superseded by the 757 – yet another Boeing success story.

**RIGHT** *Paradise Airways was a short-lived charter operator formed on the east coast of the USA in the early 1990s. Former Alaska Airlines 727-247 N324AS served with the airline for under a year in 1994/95, during which time it was photographed at New York's John F Kennedy airport*

*Founded in 1991, Miami Air also operates a fleet of seven 727-200s on ad-hoc charters. When 727-231Adv N808MA was photographed at Toronto in 1994, it had just transported the Miami Marlins baseball team (champions of the 1997 World Series) 'north of the border' to play the locally-based Blue Jays. Note the Marlins' logo specially painted on to the jet's tail*

**RIGHT** *Based at Minneapolis/St Paul, Sun Country Airlines utilises a fleet of ten 727s and five DC-10s on charter services throughout the USA. The 727s are all -200Adv aircraft, including -2J4 N284SC seen here at Gatwick in 1995 during a rare foray across the Atlantic. No stranger to London's second airport, this aircraft had originally been delivered to Sterling Airways in 1977, and later served with Dan Air*

**BELOW, RIGHT** *TWA (Trans World Airlines) has been operating the 727 since 1964, and today still owns a sizeable fleet of 39 Boeing tri-jets – including four ageing -100s. For many years the airline has struggled to survive, somehow always managing to avoid the predicted dissolution. Even in the last two years when other major US carriers have reported massive profits, TWA continues to struggle to break even. Seen decelerating after landing at Miami in January 1997 is 727-231 N54352*

RIGHT *Air Canada received the first of 39 727-233s in September 1974, the airline subsequently using the type on both domestic and cross-border services into the USA. It now has one of the largest fleets of Airbus airliners in the world, and it was the first of these – the A320 – which replaced Boeing's tri-jet in Air Canada service. Taxying to its gate at Toronto in May 1989 is C-GAAF*

**BELOW** United Airlines took delivery of its first 727 in 1964, and since then it has operated over 150 different examples of the tri-jet. Although its -100s have been disposed of, the airline still utilises 75 -200s, despite having taken delivery of a considerable number of 757s and A320s in recent years. Sporting United's current livery at Cleveland in 1995 is 727-222Adv N7271U, now in its 20th year of service

**ABOVE FAR LEFT** *Unlike in the USA, deregulation in the Canadian domestic market has been a long time coming. The granting of licences to charter airlines Air Transat and Canada 3000 to operate long-haul coast to coast services has at last brought air fares down to realistic levels. One of the newcomers into the 'open' market in 1996 was Greyhound Air, which was a subsidiary of the Greyhound Canada Transportation Corporation. The latter organisation contracted Kelowna Flightcraft to provide seven 727-200s and crews to operate services from Hamilton and Toronto to Winnipeg and Vancouver. However, mounting losses forced the parent company to abandon the project, and Greyhound Air ceased operations in the third quarter of 1997. The distinctive greyhound tail logo and toll free reservations telephone number feature prominently on 727-227Adv C-GJKF seen at Toronto*

**ABOVE LEFT** *Aero Peru currently operates three 727-100s and three -200s alongside its more modern 757. Photographed at Rio de Janeiro in October 1994, Aero Peru 727-264Adv XA-HON was on lease from Mexicana at the time*

**LEFT** *ACES Colombia (Aerolineas Centrales de Colombia SA) has recently taken delivery of four A320s, and this should see the demise of at least some of the air-line's seven-strong 727 fleet. The new Airbus jet will undoubtedly enter service on the Miami route, where 727-212Adv HK-4047-X is seen about to land in January 1997*

**BELOW** *Dominicana no longer has any aircraft of its own, instead leasing 727s, 737s and 767s from AvAtlantic, TAESA and Air Europe Italy when required. The airline used to operate a few 727s on the Santo Domingo-Miami route, including 727-2J1 HI-242-CT Duarte. This aircraft served exclusively with Dominicana for 14 years following its delivery new in 1975, but was scrapped in Costa Rica at the end of 1996*

**BELOW, FAR RIGHT** *Aeromexpress operates a pair of -200Adv aircraft, which have been converted to freighters with a large cargo door in the forward port fuselage – the door is clearly visible in this shot of 727-2K5(F)Adv N909PG about to land at Los Angeles*

**LEFT** *Mexicana has flown a considerable number of 727s over the years, yet despite the delivery of the first batch of A320s in 1991, the airline shows no signs of retiring its tri-jets. Indeed, the 20 -200Adv aircraft on-strength are fairly late-build machines with an average age of 17 years. In the early 1990s Mexicana experimented with its colour scheme by painting the tails of its aircraft in several different patterns (perhaps that's where British Airways got the idea from!?), but to ease costs and maintenance it has now standardised on the green 'tapestry' type finish as seen on 727-264Adv XA-MEZ Merida on finals to LAX in September 1996*

ABOVE As the national
carrier of the former
Yugoslavia, JAT
Jugoslovenski
Aerotransport found
itself in a similar position
to Aviogenex post-1991
(see caption opposite),
so it too leased out air-
craft and crews at
extremely cheap rates.
One airline who took
advantage of this in
1992 was British Air
Ferries, although the aircraft was soon returned
to its owner after considerable pressure was
brought to bear by com-
petitors complaining of
cheap labour and licens-
ing irregularities.
727-2H9Adv YU-AKI is
seen resting at Gatwick
in JAT livery with British
Air Ferries titles in May
1992

BELOW *Aviogenex was formed in 1968 to take advantage of the growing number of tourists visiting Yugoslavia from western Europe. However, due to the conflict in the Balkans following the splintering of the former nation in 1991, the past few years has seen the airline's fleet somewhat inactive, Aviogenex instead relying on revenue generated by leasing its aircraft to any airline it could find who would operate them. It will take many years for tourism to return to the levels achieved prior to the war, and until then the airline will have to continue looking for such leases. Seen operating a sub-charter at Gatwick during the 1997 Easter weekend is 727-2L8Adv YU-AKH. This aircraft was initially delivered to the Yugoslav Air Force, who operated it as a government VIP transport*

**BELOW RIGHT** *At the cessation of the Yugoslavian conflict, JAT slowly began to resume operations, whilst at the same time taking the opportunity to introduce a new livery to mark its relaunching. Displaying the new scheme at Heathrow in August 1996 is 727-2H9Adv YU-AKJ*

**RIGHT** *Constellation International Airlines is a Belgian charter operator which has flown a pair of 727-200s in recent years. The venerable Boeings were, however, replaced by a pair of A320s in time for the 1997 summer season. Photographed about to land on runway 02 at Brussels in August 1996 is 727-2X3Adv OO-CAH*

**ABOVE, FAR RIGHT** *Iberia has been a 727 operator since 1972 when it purchased the first of 37 aircraft. Despite having acquired a number of A320s, 757s and MD-87s during the 1990s, the Spanish airline still operates no less than 28 tri-jets. In February 1998, however, Iberia ordered a further 50 Airbus A320s, undoubtedly giving notice to its fleet of Boeing tri-jets. A trio of Iberia 727-200s are seen here at Madrid/Barajas airport's domestic terminal.*

**LEFT** *Istanbul Airlines commenced charter services in 1986 to cater for the growing tourist trade to Turkey from Western Europe. Initial equipment comprised SE 210 Caravelles, although these have now long gone in favour of an all Boeing fleet comprising 727s, 737s and 757s. Seven 727-200s are presently operated by the airline, five of which are former Lufthansa machines. 727-228 TC-AFB was photographed soon after take-off from runway 24 at Amsterdam's Schiphol airport in August 1995*

**RIGHT** *Turkish freight airline Tayfunair was formed in 1995 as a subsidiary of Cingilli Holdings. In February 1996 it acquired a former Eastern Airlines 727-225 which had earlier been converted into a freighter. Following its purchase, a twice weekly Istanbul-London/Gatwick cargo service was inaugurated by the airline, although the London destination was later switched to Stansted. However, after barely a year this service was dropped and the aircraft returned to the lessor. Photographed at Gatwick in July 1996, the aircraft in question wears the registration TC-DEL and the name Cingilli 1 on the nose*

**ABOVE, FAR RIGHT** *Serving the Turkish half of the divided island of Cyprus is the task of KTHY – Kibris Turk Hava Yollari. The airline was founded in 1974, and until recently operated aircraft lent by the Turkish national carrier THY. However, the operator has acquired some of its own equipment in the shape of four 727-200s and two A310s – aircraft types it had built up experience on when leased from THY. In 1997 the airline surprised many people when it acquired three MD-90s, although these were returned to Boeing at the end of 1997! 727-228Adv TC-JEC is taxying at Gatwick in November 1995*

**RIGHT** *Sabre Airways is a British charter airline which formed in 1994 to operate on behalf of the Goldcrest holiday group. In December that year two former Britannia Airways 737-200s were acquired, and these were subsequently joined a few months later by a pair of former Dan Air 727-200s. For the 1997 season the 737s were operated for, and in the colours of, Peach Air, while one 727 was placed in storage at the end of the year. The remaining 727 (series -276Adv G-BNNI) has been hushkitted and is seen here powering out of Gatwick in October 1997. Note the claim on the starboard nacelle – 'Boeing 727 Quiet Power'! Sabre is the premier UK customer for the Next Generation 737, having ordered four -800s*

**BELOW** *Royal Air Maroc took delivery of the first of eight 727s in 1970, all but two of which have since been disposed of. The remaining pair will no doubt be sold as soon as the airline receives the first of the 737-800s it currently has on order. 727-2B6 CN-RMQ was photographed about to land at Paris/Orly in 1992*

**ABOVE, FAR LEFT** As a long-established Danish charter airline, Sterling Airways' demise in September 1993 as a result of financial problems came as something of a surprise to the European air charter world. However, it was reborn the following year as Sterling European, its aircraft (the same 727s as had been operated by the original company) being adorned with a new livery. One of these was 727-270Adv OY-SBI, which is seen here in original Sterling colours in May 1992, but with Air Columbus titles due to a short-term lease to the Portuguese carrier

**ABOVE LEFT** Built as a 727-224Adv and delivered to Continental Airlines as N29730 in October 1973, this tri-jet was withdrawn from service and stored in Arizona in 1994. In December 1996 it was converted into a freighter through the addition of a forward cargo door, joining Sterling European two months later as OY-SEY. The jet remains in the employ of the Danish company, who operate it on behalf of, and in the colours of, TNT International. It was photographed at Stansted in April 1997 soon after entering service in its new freighter role

**RIGHT** *This immaculate winglet-equipped 727-2U5Adv served as a VIP aircraft with the Jordanian government from 1980 to 1985, when it was bought by the Brunei government. Now registered in Saudi Arabia as HZ-AB3, the jet belongs to the Al-Anwa Establishment*

**RIGHT** *Inter Air is a small South African airline which commenced services in 1994 and currently operates three elderly 727-100s on lease. The airline previously flew two slightly younger -200s leased from Safair, one of which, ZS-NOV, is seen on the Safair ramp at Johannesburg in February 1996*

**LEFT** *Ansett Australia Airlines was an early customer for the 727, only ending its partnership with the tri-jet in 1997 following a 33-year association. Ansett's 727-277 VH-RMN was photographed about to land at Sydney in March 1993 during a year-long lease to now defunct EastWest Airlines. Like an increasing number of 727s, this aircraft has since been converted into a freighter for Australian Air Express*

**BELOW LEFT** *Since delivery to Braniff in 1976 727-227 N570PE has served with five operators in the USA and two in South-East Asia. This photograph of the aircraft was taken at Bangkok during its brief four-month stint with Cambodia International Airlines in early 1995 – the aircraft displays the cheatline of previous operator Delta. The 727 is still based in Bangkok, although it now flies with Orient Express Air*

Qatar Airways was formed in 1993 to operate regional services from Doha, as well as linking the Middle Eastern country with London/Gatwick – a pair of leased A310s initially performed these flights. Due to major route expansion in 1995, a pair of former ANA 747s and four 727-200s were acquired to replace the A310s, the Boeing tri-jets being used on regional services – three of these are fitted with the JT8D-17R engines for hot/high operations. 727-2M7Adv A7-ABC was photographed as it taxied to its parking spot on the Doha ramp in September 1996. One month after this shot was taken there was a major change in the airline's management structure, which led to the acquisition of a pair of A300-600Rs, a new livery and the suspension of a number of routes

# CHAPTER 3
# Boeing 737-100 and -200

Powered by two JT8D-1 engines rated at 14,000 lb each, the prototype Boeing 737 (N73700) took-off from Renton on its maiden flight on 9 April 1967. With a gross weight of 97,800 lb, this 'baby Boeing' was capable of carrying up to 100 passengers.

Launch customer for the new 737-100 was Lufthansa, the airline having placed an order for 21 aircraft in February 1965. It took delivery of its first aircraft on 27 December 1967, the German operator christening its fleet 'City Jets' and configuring them for 84 seats – operations commenced on 10 February 1968. Later versions of the -100 were fitted with the more powerful JT8D-9, rated at 14,500 lb,

which allowed Boeing to increase the airliner's gross weight figure to 111,000 lb. The first recipient of the more powerful -100s was Malaysia-Singapore Airways (MSA). Only 30 -100s were ever built, and by January 1998 just 13 were still in use with four airlines in two countries – Peru and the USA.

No fewer than nine of these 30-year-old veterans are operated by Continental Airlines, although the airline is presently in the process of replacing them with factory-fresh 737-500s. Continental inherited 17 former Lufthansa examples when it took over People Express some years ago, whilst another two ex-German -100s

were bought by Taiwan's Far Eastern Air Transport, and were only retired in 1996. America West Airlines' large 737 fleet includes a solitary ex-MSA -100 aircraft which is used primarily to transport the Phoenix Suns basketball team across the USA from fixture to fixture! Three other MSA -100s were sold to Ansett New Zealand in 1987, but they have since been disposed of. Peruvian carriers Faucett and Aero Continente operate one and two examples respectively, the latter airline flying the world's oldest airworthy examples of the 'baby Boeing' – these aircraft were only the third and fifth examples ever built.

Other airlines which have operated the -100 second-hand include Air Cal, Air Florida, Avianca, COPA Panama, SARO and Sierra Pacific Airlines.

Even before the -100 had flown, Boeing's discussions with potential customers had revealed that a larger variant was already in demand, and thus the -200 was born. With the fuselage lengthened slightly to carry up to 130 passengers, the initial variant had a gross weight of 97,000 lb, which was subsequently increased to 117,000 lb. The speed with which the -200 was developed was quite amazing, the prototype being only the fifth 737 built. Powered by two JT8D-7B engines, this aircraft flew for the first time on 8 August 1967, with first deliveries to launch customer United Airlines taking place only two days after Lufthansa had received its first -100. United's initial order was for 40 aircraft, although it eventually acquired over 70 examples of this variant, including a number of second-hand aircraft from Frontier Airlines. United still has over 60 -200s in use, but with A319s now being

LEFT *Continental is currently the largest operator of the series -100, 17 of which were acquired following the acquisition of People Express Airlines in 1987. By the end of 1997 Continental had nine -100s still in service, although the type is being progressively withdrawn following the continuing delivery of new 737-500s. Photographed preparing to depart Buffalo Airport, New York, in 1991 is 737-130 N77215*

**ABOVE** *Alaska Airlines took delivery of its first 737-200C in 1981, and currently operates eight Combis primarily on internal Alaskan services. For these routes the aircraft are fitted with undercarriage deflectors and dissipaters beneath the engine intakes. The airline also flies two standard -200s on lease from Braathens, which are operated on behalf of ARCO and BP oil companies. Poised for touchdown on runway 14 at Anchorage in April 1996 is 737-290C N746AS*

delivered, it is now in the process of disposing of them – 26 are destined for Sempati of Indonesia.

Boeing was somewhat surprised when one of its early customers was UK-based charter airline Britannia Airways, as in those days charter operators never bought brand new aircraft. Britannia has subsequently enjoyed a long association with the 737, and at one time had 29 of the type in its inventory.

Following the success of the 727 Combi, Boeing quickly launched the -200C and QC variants in the wake of the standard -200. The first -200C flew in August 1968 and was eventually delivered to Wien Air Alaska. A total of 10 C/QC

variants were built.

Next came the -200 Advanced, in which weight-saving graphite composites were used. It also featured modifications to the leading edge slats and optional nose-wheel brakes. More powerful Pratt & Whitney engines had by this time become available (including the JT8D-17A rated at 16,000 lb), which permitted an increase in MTOW to 128,500 lb. The first flight of this variant was performed on 15 April 1971, and service entry was achieved with launch customer ANA within two months. The -200Adv proved popular, and orders continued to roll in from around the world, including 38 from Lufthansa and 35 from British Airways – half of the latter order initially served with the airline's leisure division, British Airtours. A proud moment for Boeing occurred when the 1000th 737 built – the sixth series -200Adv for Delta Airlines – was delivered in December 1983.

For those operators who wished to operate the 737 into gravel or unprepared strips, Boeing came up with some novel modifications to reduce the risk of damage to both the airframe and engines. The nose-wheel was fitted with a ski-like adapter which prevented debris from being deflected onto the underside of the fuselage, and thus causing it damage. A similar, but smaller, deflector is sited between the main wheels. Aerials fitted to the underside of the fuselage were strengthened, while the lower anti-collision light could even be retracted into the fuselage. Finally, to protect the engine a dissipater was fitted beneath the nacelle. This prod-like device projected forward underneath the intake to disturb the airflow and lessen the chance of debris being sucked in from ground level. Alaska Airlines and Air Algerie are just two of the many customers who have fitted this modification to some of their aircraft.

Despite the success of the 737 programme, and the popularity of the type with the airline community, Boeing still found time to adapt the airframe for military use. The -200 was selected by the US Air Force as a navigation trainer, this variant (with the military designation T-43A) having a strengthened floor to take the weight of the avionics consoles and suites for trainees and instructors. It also featured an additional fuel tank in the cargo compartment to extend its range.

The first T-43A flew on 10 April 1973,

and 19 were eventually delivered to the 323rd Flying Training Wing at Mather Air Force Base, California. Some of these were eventually transferred to the Air National Guard, where they were used in the transport role until eventually replaced by second-hand 727s designated as C-22Bs. Some of the T-43As are still used in the VIP transport role, whilst a number of standard -200s are now in use with other air arms as VIP or presidential transports.

Another variant developed by Boeing was a maritime surveillance version known as the Surveiller. This featured two antennae on the upper rear fuselage for a high resolution side-looking radar. Only three such aircraft were sold, all to the Indonesian Air Force (TNI-AU).

The 1114th, and final, -200 was delivered to Xiamen Airlines in August 1988.

**ABOVE, FAR LEFT** *Aircraft of Frontier Airlines are amongst the most sought after by aviation enthusiasts, the reason being that each aircraft features a large painting of an indigenous American animal on each side of its tail. This 737-201 (N217US) was acquired from USAir in 1994, and is one of seven of the type currently on strength. It features a mountain lion on the port side of the fin and an eagle on the starboard, and was photographed about to depart Phoenix, Arizona, for its base at Denver, Colorado, in April 1997*

**ABOVE LEFT** *USAir, which changed its name to US Airways early in 1997, is now in the process of disposing of some of its older 737-200s, a number of which were inherited during the take-over of Piedmont Airlines. Photographed on the taxyway at Buffalo airport, New York State, in June 1995 is 737-2B7 N284US*

**LEFT** *Aloha Airlines 737-200 N726AL turns onto final approach for Honolulu in January 1993*

**BELOW RIGHT** *The 737 fleet of El Salvador's TACA International Airlines has expanded considerably in recent years, and currently numbers 10 -200s and five -300s. The airline has also increased the number of services to Miami, where 737-205 N235TA was photographed in January 1997*

**BELOW, FAR RIGHT** *Brazilian carriers Rio Sul, TransBrasil and Varig all operate a number of new generation 737-300s, -400s or -500s. VASP, however, has stuck faithfully to its older -200s, 22 of which are in use, although a pair of -300s are used on the Rio/Santos Dumont-Sao Paulo/Congonhas 'air bridge' route. Most of the airline's -200s have been acquired from a number of sources, and include a handful of 29-year-old veterans, although the aircraft featured here – 737-2A1 PP-SMF – was delivered new to VASP in 1972*

**LEFT** *Air Malta received its first 737 back in 1983, and currently operates a pair of -200s and three -300s. Two A320s complete the inventory, with its previous quartet of Avro RJ70s having recently been transferred to Italian subsidiary Azzurra Air. Photographed on departure from Gatwick, bound for Malta's Luqa airport, in December 1997 is 737-2Y5 9H-ABE, which was delivered new to the airline exactly ten years before*

**OPPOSITE** *British Airways 737-236 G-BKYJ Touchstone is seen climbing out of its Gatwick base at the start of a morning flight in March 1998*

**ABOVE LEFT** *British Airways introduced its new livery, comprising a number of multi-cultural tail logos, in June 1997, and despite a less than favourable reception from the airline's staff, it has proved a big hit with aviation enthusiasts! One of the most popular schemes to date is the 'Benyhone'/'Mountain of the Birds' tartan scheme, which now adorns a number of different types ranging in size from the BN-2 Islander to the 747-400. One of the first recipients of this scheme was 737-236 G-BGDL, seen here in September 1997 departing Gatwick*

**LEFT** *The 'Benyhone' scheme has been nicknamed the travel rug by British Airways personnel, and is featured on more aircraft types than any other scheme. In this shot it adorns 737-236 G-BGDL and British Regional BAe 146-200 G-GNTZ, parked at Gatwick's North Terminal*

**RIGHT** *The new collection of tail logos has provoked numerous, and mixed, responses from both industry and the public at large, with the most openly vociferous and hostile criticism coming from the latter quarter. Certainly the majority of the airline's workforce do not seem enamoured by it, particularly the pilots, who have to put up with some interesting 'comments' on radio frequencies. This scheme, seen on 737-236 G-BGDR, has an Irish flavour, and is known as 'Colum', which is Gaelic for Dove*

**ABOVE, CENTRE**
*Following the country's independence from the Soviet Union, Lithuanian Airlines was quick to acquire a leased 737-200 to operate some of the newly inaugurated routes to western European capitals. Former Malev 737-2Q8 was leased from Guiness-Peat in December 1991 and appropriately registered LY-GPA. The initial livery featured a bright green cheatline, but this has since been dropped in favour of this predominantly red and white scheme. The airline now has three 737s*

LEFT *The success of easyJet, Britain's first true low-cost no-frills airline, has probably surprised many in the industry, not least British Airways, which has enjoyed something of a monopoly on most domestic routes. One of the reasons for easyJet's success is probably its choice of Luton airport as a base. It is a low-cost venue from which to operate, serving a large catchment area which includes north London, and proving easily accessible by various modes of transport. Although it started operations with a pair of leased 737-200s, easyJet now operates six series -300s and has a further 12 new examples on order. The airline's first aircraft, G-BECG, is seen here taxying for departure at its Luton base in June 1996*

LEFT *Olympic Airways received the first of 11 737-200s in 1976, the fleet subsequently being supplemented by seven -400s in 1991. More recently, the airline announced an order for eight series -800s, which will at last allow its elderly 727s to be retired. 737-284 SX-BCF Poseidon was seen at Geneva in March 1996 featuring the airline's current livery, which has a lighter shade of blue than was previously worn*

**RIGHT** *Transaero Airlines is a successful independent Russian carrier which was formed in 1990. In 1993 a pair of 737-200s were acquired on lease, followed by a further three ex-British Airways examples. These have since been joined by 757s and DC-10s, and the airline's network now includes Bangkok, Hong Kong and Los Angeles. Two of the 737s are operated jointly with Latvian carrier Riair, and bear Latvian registrations and the titles of both airlines. Amongst the routes flown are a daily Moscow-Riga-London/Gatwick service. At Gatwick in October 1997 is 737-236 YL-BAC*

**RIGHT** *Irish carrier Ryanair began operations in 1985 as the first real competition for Aer Lingus. Initial equipment comprised ATR-42 and BAC One-Eleven aircraft, with services from provincial Irish airports to Luton. The airline's fleet is now comprised solely of 737-200s, 19 of which are in use flying between 13 destinations in the UK and its London terminus at Stansted. The airline has recently followed Western Pacific's lead by painting several of its aircraft as advertising billboards, the first for Jaguar Cars. Illustrated rotating from Gatwick's runway is 737-230 EI-CNW, one of six ex-Lufthansa machines which joined the fleet in 1997*

LEFT *Air Ukraine International Airlines was formed in 1992 with a pair of 737s to serve several western European destinations. It soon transpired that there was confusion outside of the Ukraine as to the airline's identity, as Air Ukraine – the former Kiev directorate of Aeroflot – had a very similar livery and logo. To remedy this, the newcomer changed its name to Ukraine International Airlines and adopted a new logo. In its short lifespan the company has operated the 737-200, -300 and -400, and it has a further two -400s and one -300 on order, which will presumably replace the pair of -200s it currently leases. The latter include former Chinese 737-247 UR-GAC, seen here at London/Gatwick in July 1997*

**ABOVE** To cover a short-age of capacity, Ukraine International has leased Aviogenex 737-2K3 YU-ANP since the spring of 1997, the aircraft retaining its former livery apart from Ukraine International titles and tail logo

**BELOW, FAR LEFT**
Based at Chongqing, Air Great Wall is just one of the many new airlines which have sprung up in China during the last few years. This airline was formed in 1992, and operates a fleet of two Tu-154s and three 737-200s – the latter all served with CAAC and then Air China, before joining Air Great Wall in 1995. Photographed waiting to depart Beijing's Capital airport in March 1997 is 737-2T4 B-2507

**BELOW LEFT** Boeing 737-2T4 B-2516 served with both CAAC and China Southwest Airlines before joining Xiamen Airlines in 1992. Like many Chinese carriers, Xiamen Airlines' fleet is comprised solely of Boeing products, namely the 737 and 757. The former includes five -200s and seven -500s

**BELOW** *South African Airways has employed the 737-200 on domestic services for 30 years, although the 13 aircraft currently in use are rather more youthful, with the oldest being built in 1981. The 737s are supplemented by a fleet of A300s and A320s on domestic and regional routes and four 747 variants used on intercontinental destinations. The airline introduced a new livery in 1997 which is based on the country's new flag, and differs considerably from the old scheme seen on 737-244 ZS-SIL Wilge at Johannesburg in March 1996*

**LEFT** *Air Algerie's jet fleet has remained unchanged for many years, comprising 727s, 737s and 767s, as well as four A310s. Despite its short-haul fleet of 11 727s and 15 737s now all being well over 20 years old, the airline has appeared to be in no great hurry to look for a successor. The aircraft featured here, 7T-VES, is one of two -2D6 Combi variants in service*

**BELOW LEFT** *Air Sinai, which was initially formed as a one-aircraft outfit in 1982, is a sub-sidiary of Egyptair. The airline's sole 737-2N7 SU-GAN has served since 1986, and is seen about to land at Athens in November 1990. The company has recently doubled its fleet by leas-ing a 737-500 from Egyptair*

**RIGHT** *Air New Zealand (ANZ) currently operates a fleet of some 36 Boeing aircraft, namely the 737, 767 and 747 Due to its geographical location, the 12-strong 737-200 fleet fulfils purely domestic requirements. For some time Air New Zealand has been expected to place orders for new and next generation 737s, and is still likely to do so yet. This pair of ANZ 737-200s, photographed during a turnaround at Christchurch in November 1996, still sport the airline's old livery, as the new one had only just been introduced at the time. The airline's 737s are all named in Maori after indigenous birds, the aircraft nearest the camera being the hushkitted -204 ZK-NAA Parekareka (Spotted Shag). This aircraft began its career with Britannia Airways in 1982*

**RIGHT** *Taiwan's Far Eastern Air Transport began operations in 1957, and the first of the 11 737s which it operated joined the company in 1976 – this number included a pair of former Lufthansa -100s. By the end of 1997 only two 737s remained in the inventory, and their disposal was imminent as the airline's MD-80 fleet has risen to ten aircraft. Three 757s complete the fleet, with a further five on order. Seen waiting to depart Taipei's busy Sungshan domestic airport in September 1995 is 737-2Q8 B-2615, this aircraft having been delivered new to FAT in 1979, and being one of the two still in use in 1997*

**BELOW RIGHT** *An aircraft rarely, if ever, seen outside South-East Asia is Lao Aviation's sole 737-200. The airline has operated three examples of the type, including 737-291 RDPL-34125, which flew between 1993 and 1996. It is seen here taxying for departure at Bangkok in March 1995, bound for the Laotian capital Vientiane*

**BELOW, FAR RIGHT** *Air New Zealand's current livery was unveiled in the summer of 1996, and is seen at Wellington on 737-219 ZK-NAX Piere (the Maori name for the New Zealand Robin)*

# Chapter 4
# Boeing 737-300, -400 and -500

The New Generation series 737s have a number of attributes that the series -200 does not have, the most significant of these being the increase in performance through the fitment of noticeably quieter, and more fuel efficient, engines. The powerplant that confers all of these advantages is the General Electric CFM56-3B, which is available in three variants rated at 18,500 lb, 20,000 lb and 22,000 lb – these were installed on early production examples of the of -500, -300 and -400 respectively. Later, when the CFM56-3C (rated at 25,000 lb) became available, this became the preferred powerplant selected by most customers for all three New Generation types.

The prototype -300 was the 1001st 737 built, and it lifted off from Renton's compact runway on its maiden flight on 24 February 1984. Launch customers were USAir and Southwest with orders for 10 each, plus options on 20 more. Southwest has since become the best customer for the -300, and the 737 in general. The airline took delivery of its 186th, and last, -300 only a matter of weeks before taking delivery of its first series 700. The next customer for the New Generation 737 was Piedmont Airlines, which was taken over by USAir in 1987, substantially adding to the latter's 737 inventory. Over the next two years a number of smaller US carriers also took delivery of -300s.

1987 also saw the 737-300 join the ranks of some of America's largest carriers due to a rash of take-overs. American, Continental and Delta all inherited -300s as Air California, New York Air and Western Airlines respectively were subsumed into the larger carriers. Another major US operator in the shape of United Airlines also has a large fleet of -300s, 101

**LEFT** *Continental Airlines has a large 737 fleet numbering some 150 aircraft, with a further 20 series -500s in the process of being delivered – the balance of an order for 67. As these -500s are delivered the airline will finally dispense with the services of its remaining -100s, while 17 series -200s and 65 -300s complete the 737 inventory. Continental also has 78 Next Generation 737s on order – 30 each of the -600 and -800 and 18 -700s. Seen in the airline's current livery, 737-3TO N12318 taxies for departure from its Cleveland hub in May 1995*

**LEFT** *America West has steadily expanded its route network in recent years, utilising a fleet of 737s, 757s and A320s. The 737 fleet comprises examples of the -100, -200 and -300, with the latter variant proving numerically superior with over 40 aircraft. During the 1996/97 winter the airline introduced a new livery, although it is the old scheme which is shown here on 737-353 N315AW seen on approach to Orange County airport in September 1996. This aircraft previously served with Air Europe*

**ABOVE** *Photographed on approach to Los Angeles in 1995 is Delta Airlines 737-347 N311WA. The registration suffix identifies this as one of 13 -300s (and a similar number of -200s) inherited from the take-over of Western Airlines in 1987. Added to its own -200s, the airline had 54 examples of this later variant in service in 1997, Delta also being an early customer for the Next Generation variants with an order for 70 of the series -800*

of which have so far been delivered. Phoenix-based America West Airlines has increased its quota of -300s to 42, while recently-defunct Western Pacific operated its fleet as 'logo-jets', painted in the colours of anyone who would pay the required amount to have their logo or markings displayed on the aircraft.

The -300's success has not been confined to the USA, however, as the type is now in widespread service across the globe, and especially in Europe, where the type has proven popular with the region's many charter airlines, as well as scheduled carriers. An example of the new breed of European operator using the -300 is low-cost, no frills, airline easyJet, which has recently ordered a batch of 12 new

machines to add to the six it already flies.

It was a -300 which enabled the 737 to enter the record books as the world's most successful aircraft when the 1833rd example was rolled out at Renton on 19 February 1990, destined for British Midland Airways.

The -300 has also enjoyed success in the People's Republic of China, where it is now in use with no less than 15 operators – more than in any other country, including the USA. A number of other Asian carriers operate the series -300 too, including Malaysia and Singapore, who have also purchased freighter variants fitted with a side cargo door. In contrast to other world markets, sales to African carriers have been rather slow, although Kenya Airways acquired two -300s in 1997 to replace its venerable -200s. Still in the southern hemisphere, the Brazilian operators TransBrasil, Varig and VASP all operate the -300, but elsewhere in the continent it is the elderly -200 which predominates.

'Down under', Ansett Australia took delivery of the first of 16 examples in 1986, whilst Trans Australia Airlines ordered a similar number which are now operated in Qantas livery. Some of the nearby South Pacific operators such as AirCalin, Air Pacific, Polynesian and Royal Tongan Airlines also operate one or two examples apiece.

By the end of January 1998 total orders for the -300 had reached an impressive 1122, thus making it the most popular of all 737 variants by surpassing the 1114 figure for the -200.

Piedmont Airlines, an early customer for the -300, became the launch customer for the -400 with an order in June 1986 for 25 aircraft, plus options on a further 30.

BELOW LEFT *Dallas-based Southwest Airlines is the world's largest 737 operator, having 261 such aircraft in its inventory at the end of 1997. These comprise 47 -200s, 186 -300s, 25 -500s and the first three of 129 -700s on order. Southwest's busiest hub is Phoenix, Arizona, where 737-3H4 N629SW was snapped taxiing to its gate in April 1997. This aircraft has an all-silver fuselage to commemorate the airline's silver anniversary, complete with a stylised heart-shaped '25' on the nose*

RIGHT *Southwest Airlines 737-3H4 N609SW in 'California One' colours at Phoenix in April 1997, this scheme featuring a wraparound rendition of the state flag on its fuselage and engine nacelles*

BELOW *The low slung CFM56 engines fitted to the 737-300 give little ground clearance, despite the flattened underside of the cowling. Southwest Airlines 737s (including N6645W seen here in April 1997) feature the figure '1' in a red heart to signify good service awards presented to the airline by the US travelling public*

USAir also signalled its intention to take the -400 into its fleet, its final purchase being dramatically swelled when it acquired Piedmont – this corporate buy out swelled USAir's 737 fleet to a staggering 240 aircraft. Despite the success of the -300 in the USA, sales of the -400 in the home market remained stagnant until 1992 when Alaska Airlines and Markair 'joined the club'. That same year Carnival Airlines took delivery of the first of seven it had ordered, although towards the end of 1997 these aircraft started to appear in Pan American colours as the revived carrier has amalgamated with Carnival. In 1992 Hawaiian-based Aloha Airlines briefly operated a pair of -400s, although these have since been disposed of. Five

years were to pass before the next -400 delivery to a US customer, which saw newly-launched Pro Air receiving two aircraft in 1997.

The -400 has proved much more popular in Europe, however, and it was new charter airline Air UK Leisure who became the first overseas customer for this version. It has since become the workhorse of many European charter airlines, as well as major national carriers like British Airways, KLM and THY. The 1000th New Generation 737 built was the first of a batch of 24 for British Airways, being delivered to the airline in October 1991. Lufthansa received 11 aircraft in 1992, but these aircraft somehow seemed too large for the airline's predominantly small-capacity 737 fleet and most were soon leased out. They were subsequently disposed of in 1997.

The type has also found a place in the fleets of four established eastern European airlines which had previously been dominated by Ilyushin and Tupolev types — namely CSA, LOT, Malev and Ukraine International. Even Aeroflot has recognised its worth and is about to take delivery of ten aircraft. Unlike the -300, only a handful of the larger -400s are in use in China, although a major boost for the aircraft came from Asia in the form of an order for 40 examples for Malaysia Airlines, who took delivery of the first of these in April 1992. The -400 is also in use with Asiana Airlines in the Republic of Korea, Garuda Indonesia, Japan Airlines and Thai International. In Taiwan China Airlines took delivery of six aircraft in 1997 to replace its -200s on domestic services, as well as supplement A300s on selected regional routes.

In Australia 16 aircraft were delivered to Australian Airlines during 1989/90, although these are now operated in the colours of the national carrier Qantas, which has since increased the fleet to 22 aircraft. Elsewhere in the region, small carriers like Air Nauru, Air Vanuatu and Solomons Airlines have also operated single examples. Despite the size of the continent, the only customer in South America has been TransBrasil, whilst in Africa the type is flown exclusively by Royal Air Maroc and Egyptian charter operator AMC. The total order figure to date for the -400 is considerably lower than the -300, standing at 481 at 31 January 1998, 36 of which are still to be delivered.

The remaining, and last, New Generation variant to be launched was the -500, which was designed specifically to fulfil a demand made by numerous airlines for a modern, updated, version of the -200. The maiden flight of the prototype was completed on 30 June 1989, with launch customers Braathens and Southwest receiving their first examples eight months later. In America, United Airlines received 57 aircraft, some of which have been operated in Shuttle colours — United's low cost division. Continental Airlines is the only other American customer for the type, having ordered 67 aircraft. The last of these is due for delivery in 1999, thus allowing the airline to finally dispose of its remaining veteran -100s.

Once again it is European carriers who have dominated the sales figures for the -500, with both established and new-born airlines ordering the variant. The Scandinavian market in particular has

**BELOW RIGHT** *A subsidiary of Varig, Rio Sul Airlines was formed in 1976. In recent years its fleet has significantly increased in size, with Embraer EMB-120 Brasilias and Fokker 50s being used on regional routes. In 1997 the airline received its first Embraer RJ-145 regional jet, which will supplement the 10-strong 737-500 fleet. The latter type was introduced in October 1992 with the delivery of 737-5YO PT-SLN, seen here at Sao Paulo's downtown Congonhas airport in October 1994*

proven to be a fertile hunting ground for Boeing's salesmen, with Maersk Air and Linjeflyg ordering the -500 in significant numbers. However, in 1993 Linjeflyg was taken over by SAS who, after operating the type for only a short time, handed the entire fleet over to British Midland. Lufthansa made it a 'full house' of 737 variants when it ordered the -500, and to date it is the only airline to have operated every type of 'baby Boeing' from the -100 through to the -500. The German national carrier has 30 -500s, one of which (D-ABIK) was the 2000th 737 built and, coincidentally, the 100th for Lufthansa. It was delivered to the airline in February 1991. German charter airline Hapag Lloyd also utilises this variant.

Ireland's Aer Lingus (which operated every model of 737 apart from the -100) has taken delivery of 10 aircraft, Air France received the first of 18 in 1991 and Sabena completed a 'hat-trick' of New Generation types with an order for six -500s soon after. In eastern Europe, Balkan Bulgarian became the first customer to order the -500, followed by CSA and LOT.

Despite the success of other variants in the Asian market, sales of the -500 have proven very sluggish, with only a handful being sold to Asiana and Xiamen Airlines. More recently, ANA received the first of 14 examples in 1995, whilst Garuda has five on order.

In North Africa there has been success with all three major carriers in the region, Egyptair, Royal Air Maroc and Tunisair operating the variant in small numbers. Elsewhere in the vast continent, Uganda Airlines has so far been the sole customer, a solitary aircraft being delivered in July 1995.

New Brazilian airline Rio Sul received its first example in October 1992, and its fleet will soon include 12 such aircraft. At the moment the only other Latin American operators are the Chilean and Peruvian Air Forces, both of whom have one aircraft for VIP duties. Total orders for the -500 currently stand at 383, 356 of which have been delivered to date.

Despite the early success of the Next Generation programme (particularly the -700 and -800), Boeing has stated that it will continue to produce the -300, -400 and -500 series as long as a demand exists from its global customer base; which would seem logical.

**LEFT** *Western Pacific Airlines began operation at Colorado Springs in April 1995 with 737-300s, and very soon the airline's aircraft achieved global fame due to the innovative idea of turning their jets into 'mobile billboards'. The airline not only gained significant revenue from the customer who wanted to advertise its product on the aircraft, but the high profile schemes made everyone aware of just who Western Pacific was – normally an airline would have to pay a hefty fee to an advertising agency to gain such recognition! Despite enjoying such a raised profile, Western Pacific endured financial difficulties throughout 1997, and at one time a merger with Frontier Airlines looked on the cards. However, this failed to come to fruition and the airline ended 1997 under Chapter 11 bankruptcy protection. This innovative airline finally ceased operations in early February 1998. Advertising the Broadmoor Colorado ski resort hotel, 737-3B7 N947WP is climbing out of Phoenix Sky Harbor airport in April 1997*

**RIGHT** Air Europa was formed in 1986 as a subsidiary of Britain's Air Europe, the airline quickly taking advantage of the growing tourist trade visiting the Spanish mainland and islands. Despite its parent company's demise in the early 1990s, Air Europa has continued operations, which now include some scheduled services, both international and domestic. To cope with its increased flying schedule, the airline's fleet has expanded considerably in recent years to comprise 12 737-300s and six -400s – it also utilises five 757s and a single 767. 737-4YO EC-GAZ was photographed taxying from the domestic terminal at Madrid/Barajas airport in September 1997

**RIGHT** Brazil's national carrier Varig introduced a new livery in 1997, although this shot of 737-3K9 PP-VNY at Rio de Janeiro Galeao international airport in 1994 illustrates the old scheme – note the Varig DC-10 landing in the background. The airline currently operates 28 -300s (with a further three on order) alongside 17 considerably older -200s

ABOVE Like many airlines in eastern Europe, Balkan Bulgarian has looked westwards for some if its new equipment. Although having not totally forsaken its Russian-built equipment (it still operates a considerable number of Tu-154s as well as An-24s), Balkan commenced a leasing deal for three 737-500s in 1990/91, followed by two 767s in 1992. The airline's first 737-53A, LZ-BOA City of Sofia, is seen on approach to runway 02 at Brussels in August 1996

**BELOW** *The British travelling public have much to thank British Midland Airways (BMA) for, as this independent carrier has forced British Airways to drastically lower fares on routes it previously enjoyed a monopoly on – a factor applicable to both domestic and European destinations. Seen wearing British Midland's old livery at Edinburgh's Turnhouse airport in November 1993 is 737-33A G-OBMC. The towers of the Forth Road Bridge are clearly visible in the upper right background*

**LEFT** *Norwegian carrier Braathens has been a 737 operator since 1971, its two remaining -200s having been leased out to allow the company to utilise its new generation fleet of 737s on an expanding route network. The airline now operates 24 -500s and seven -400s, with 12 -700s remaining on order – the first of these should have been delivered by the summer of 1998. Photographed soon after rotation from London/Gatwick in December 1997 is 737-405 LN-BRE, christened Hakon V Magnusson*

**BELOW LEFT** *For several years now Braathens has painted up an aircraft in Sommerflyet markings to mark the start of summer after a long, cold and dark winter. 737-505 LN-BRJ has been the aircraft chosen for the past few years, and it is seen here at Gatwick in 1995 in a scheme devised by Norwegian school children*

**RIGHT** *British Airways
has long been one of
Boeing's most faithful
customers, and it was no
surprise when the airline
ordered the 737-400 for
its European route net-
work. The company
currently has 34 exam-
ples of this variant (20
of which are based at
Gatwick), including several leased aircraft it
inherited following the
acquisition of Dan Air.
'BA's' Gatwick-based
737-400 fleet continues
to expand, and it
includes 737-436 G-
DOCZ, which is seen
preparing to depart
Gatwick for Madrid in
July 1997. This particular
aircraft was re-registered
G-BVBZ prior to being
delivery to the airline,
who immediately placed
it in storage at Mojave
in October 1993 due to
over-capacity. It then
spent seven months on
lease to Air Europa,
before finally joining the
'BA' fleet in December
1994*

**OPPOSITE, BELOW**
*In 1997 British Midland
painted additional 'The
Airline for Europe' titles
on the upper fuselage of
its aircraft – seen here
on 737-3Q8 G-OBMP
during a rare visit to
Gatwick in August of
that year, where the air-
craft was operating on
behalf of CityFlyer due
to the latter airline expe-
riencing a shortage of
capacity*

**ABOVE** In 1997 British Midland introduced a new livery which, at first glance, is not unlike that worn by the aircraft of US partner United Airlines. The airline has a large fleet of 737-300s, -400s and -500s, numbering nine, six and 13 respectively, with most of the latter on lease from another partner, SAS. In 1997 BMA announced an order for A320s and A321s, although some of the 737s will still remain in use following the delivery of the European airliners. Photographed sporting the new livery on approach to Heathrow in August 1997 is 737-33A G-OBMJ

**LEFT** *Dan Air had been steadily building up its fleet of new generation 737s prior to its November 1992 take-over by British Airways – a number of industry observers stated that had it made the switch from fuel-thirsty BAC One-Elevens and 727s to modern 737s earlier, it would not have found itself in the financial difficulties that led to its downfall. 737-4S3 G-BVNN was seen at its Gatwick base in May 1992*

**RIGHT** *Former German commuter airline Delta Air was taken over by British Airways in 1992, the British operator renaming its new subsidiary Deutsche BA. The airline operates mainly German domestic services, and has recently increased its frequency on most routes as it battles for supremacy with Lufthansa. It also operates to London/Gatwick from Hamburg and Munich, but has dropped its services from Berlin and Bremen. Seen at Gatwick in August 1995 is 737-3L9 D-ADBC, one of ten leased from Maersk Air*

**RIGHT** *Deutsche BA is in the process of taking delivery of new 737-300s from Boeing, allowing its leased Fokker 100s to be returned to owner's TAT. In line with the adoption of British Airways' new global livery, Deutsche BA's aircraft have been allocated four different schemes, namely 'Edelweiss', 'Metropolis', 'Schrifttanz' and 'Sterntaler'. The latter is German for 'Fairy Tale', and is seen on brand new 737-300 D-ADBL at Gatwick in December 1997. This scheme has also been applied to at least two 'BA' aircraft, whose crews have nicknamed it 'Pavement Pizza'*

**ABOVE** *As Britain's first true low-cost carrier, easyJet commenced operations from Luton in 1995 with a pair of leased 737-200s. These have since been disposed of in favour of six leased -300s, and the airline placed an order with Boeing for a further 12 in 1997. Having started operations from Luton to the Scottish destinations of Aberdeen, Edinburgh and Glasgow, easyJet has since added Inverness to its list of domestic routes. It has also expanded its European operations to include Barcelona, Geneva, Palma, Amsterdam and Nice, the latter two destinations also being served from a new hub at Liverpool. 737-300 G-EZYC is seen taxying for departure at Glasgow in August 1997*

**RIGHT** *Following Estonia's independence from the former Soviet Union, Estonian Air was formed in 1991 using ex-Aeroflot Tu-134s and Yak-40s. These types have been progressively withdrawn following the acquisition of two new 737-500s and a pair of Fokker 50s, all of which are leased. The airline's 737s are used on daily services from Tallinn to Amsterdam, Copenhagen and London/Gatwick, the latter airport being the venue for this photograph of 737-5Q8 ES-ABC, taken in July 1997*

**BELOW RIGHT** *Futura International Airways is yet another Spanish charter airline formed specifically to cater for the booming tourist trade. In 1997 it also started limited scheduled services, including a thrice weekly Palma-London/Gatwick service. Sole equipment is the 737-400, 11 of which are currently used. Photographed at Gatwick in October 1996 is 737-4YO EC-EVE, which has been with airline since being built in 1990*

BELOW *The Polish national carrier LOT Polskie Linie Lotnicze has gone further than any other eastern European carrier in modernising its fleet, which is now solely comprised of modern Western types – ATR-72s, 737s and 767s. The 737 fleet is made up of seven -400s and six -500s, although three series -300s were also used in the summer of 1997 to cater for a shortage of capacity. Photographed in October 1997 on approach to Gatwick, inbound from Krakow, is 737- 55D SP-LKF*

ABOVE *During 1997 Maersk Air took delivery of a new batch of 737-500s, permitting some of its older 'baby Boeings' to be transferred to its UK subsidiary, and British Airways franchise carrier. In the spring of 1998 the airline will receive the first of six -700s. Poised for touchdown on Gatwick's runway in October 1997 is 1996-build 737-5L9 OY-APD, sporting the airline's tranquil pale blue livery*

BELOW LEFT *Lufthansa is in the unique position of having operated every 737 variant from the series -100 through to the -500. It has not, however, yet ordered any of the Next Generation variants, its requirement in this arena seemingly being filled by Airbus Industrie with its A319, A320 and A321. Lufthansa is slowly disposing of its -200s, as it has already done with its -400s. The airline's 737 inventory now comprises 47 -300s and 30 -500s, one of the latter variant, 737-530 D-ABIM Salzgitter, photographed taxying at Berlin/Tegel in May 1997*

**RIGHT** *Malev Hungarian Airlines has progressively introduced Western aircraft into its fleet, although it still operates a small number of Tu-134s and -154s. The airline's 737 fleet now numbers 12 aircraft, comprising six -200s, four -300s and two -400s. 737- 3YO HA-LED is seen in March 1994 at Budapest's Ferihegy airport taxying past a type that it has progressively replaced. Note the unusual, but distinctive, control tower building in the background*

**BELOW RIGHT**
*Sabena Belgian World Airlines has been operating the 727 since 1967 and the 737 since 1974. Its complement of the latter type presently including examples of the -200, -300, -400 and -500 – six of the latter variant are used by the Belgian carrier, including OO-SYG which was seen at Brussels in 1995 with a 'Flying together with Swissair' sticker on the rear fuselage. The airline has ordered A320s to replace some of its 737s*

**LEFT** *Monarch Airlines has operated the 737 since 1980, its fleet including a number of series -300 aircraft operated on behalf of, and in the colours of, EuroBerlin France. Monarch finally disposed of its last 737-300 to easyJet in April 1997. Photographed at Gatwick in 1994 is 737-33A G-MONV, this aircraft still being regularly seen at Gatwick as OY-MBN of Maersk Air*

LEFT *Brussels based Virgin Express was formed when Virgin boss Richard Branson acquired a major stake in Euro Belgian Airlines, resulting in a change of strategy and a new name. The carrier now operates predominantly scheduled services, including flights to London's Gatwick and Heathrow airports on behalf of Sabena. The airline has helped to pioneer low cost services from Brussels to other European cities, the company adopting a reverse livery to that worn by Virgin Atlantic aircraft The high profile bright red fuselage and white fin are perfectly illustrated in this view of 737-3M8 OO-LTL seen climbing out of Gatwick in December 1997*

**RIGHT** *China Southern Airlines' 737 fleet is even larger than that of Air China, with 23 series -300s and 11 -500s presently in use. The airline also has a large fleet of 757s, and was the first Chinese operator of the 777. It had been expected that China Southern would have opted for the Next Generation series of 737s, although this now seems unlikely as the airline has taken delivery of a number of A320s. Illustrated is 737-31B B-2941*

**LEFT** *Photographed in uncharacteristically clear British skies, Tarom 737-38J YR-BGE bears the name of Romanian town Timisoara. Although the airline has five examples of this aircraft on strength, it operates a generally ageing and convoluted fleet comprised of An-24s, Il-18s, licence-built BAC One-Elevens, Tu-154s, Il-62s and even 707s. It also has a pair of A310s, a third example having been written-off*

**BELOW LEFT** *Due to the ever increasing demand for air travel in China, most of the country's airlines have been steadily increasing the size of their fleets, with the 737 becoming a firm local favourite. National carrier Air China presently has 19 737-300s, and in January 1998 announced an order for five series -800s. Seen taxying for departure at Beijing/Capital airport, 737-3J6 B-2587 was photographed in March 1997*

ABOVE *During 1997 China Yunnan Airlines added a further four 737-300s to its fleet, which now stands at 14 – the company also has three 767s. From its base at Kunming, in Yunnan Province, the airline operates throughout China and also to some regional Asian destinations including Bangkok, where 737-341 B-2594 was photographed in 1995. Note the titles YUNNAN AIRLINES – the China prefix has since been added*

LEFT *Shenzhen Airlines is another of China's smaller carriers. It is named after the Shenzhen Special Administrative Region which shares its southern border with Hong Kong. This airline is another equipped solely with the 737-300, six of which are currently used. The aircraft featured here, 737-3Q8 B-2971 served with Ladeco in Chile for four years prior to being taken on charge by its present operator in 1996.*

BELOW LEFT *Many of China's smaller airlines are named after the cities or provinces in which there are based. For example, Shandong Airlines is named after the province of the same name and based in the city of Jinan. The company has a fleet of just one Yun-7 turboprop and three 737-35N aircraft, the latter all being delivered in 1996. Three 737-800s are on order, although whether they are to replace or supplement the -300s is not yet known. A twice daily service to Beijing is operated, where B-2961 was photographed in March 1997*

**RIGHT** *Malaysia Airlines currently has 53 New Generation 737s in its inventory, although some of these are leased out to other regional carriers. The size of the order for the New Generation types surprised many, effectively more than doubling the airline's fleet of 'baby Boeings'. The 737 inventory includes a pair of 737-3H6(F) freighters which were converted into the cargo role from new, the aircraft featuring a large forward loading door. These jets are operated by the airline's MASkargo division, and are used on a daily Kuala Lumpur-Hong Kong flight, as well as on other local routes. Photographed on approach to Hong Kong in November 1994 is 9M-MZB*

**RIGHT** *Operating alongside two Yun-7 turboprops with Zhongyuan Airlines are a trio of 737-37K aircraft which were delivered in 1994. Like most of China's smaller operators, Zhongyuan Airlines' primary routes are to the major cities of Beijing, Guanghzou and Shanghai. Aircraft B-2935 is seen on a regular visit to the capital in March 1997*

ABOVE *China Xinhua Airlines began operations from Beijing in early 1993 with a single 737-300. The 'baby Boeing' is still the only type operated, although six series -300s and three -400s are now in use. 737-39K B-2934 was delivered in August 1994 and is seen about to depart Beijing's Capital airport*

**RIGHT** *Polynesian Airlines' association with the 737 dates back to 1981 when it operated a leased -200, which served until 1987. It currently flies 737-3Q8 5W-ILF, which was delivered new in 1992 and, as the registration might suggest, is leased from ILFC – the aircraft bears the name Tooa, and is seen at Auckland in March 1993*

**BELOW, FAR LEFT**
Australian Airlines was acquired by Qantas in October 1993, and the carrier's A300s and 737-300s (16 -300s and an equal number of -400s) were duly incorporated into the national carrier's fleet. Photographed on approach to Sydney in February 1993 is the airline's first 737-376, VH-TAF

**BELOW LEFT**
Photographed at Auckland with additional Royal Tongan titles is Solomons Airlines 737-4Q8 H4-SOL, which was operated for two years until transferred to Qantas in 1994. Royal Tongan now operates a -300 jointly with Air Pacific, whilst Solomons also uses a -300 on its services to Australia, New Zealand and the Pacific Islands from Honiara

# CHAPTER 5
# Boeing 737-600, -700, -800 and -900

When Boeing announced the launch of the Next Generation 737 on 17 November 1993, it was not long before orders started rolling in, particularly for the -700 and -800.

Of the three variants announced, the -600 was the last to be developed. Built to replace the -500, the aircraft is only a few inches longer, and has the same capacity (108-132 seats). The launch customer was SAS Scandinavian Airlines who, in March 1995, announced an order for 35 aircraft, which they later increased to 41. This came as something of a surprise to industry observers, for SAS has been a loyal McDonnell Douglas customer for near on three decades, operating the largest MD-80 fleet outside the USA, and at the time had orders in hand for the MD-90, which are currently being delivered. While sales of the -700 and -800 have flourished, orders for the -600 have been virtually static.

Then Continental Airlines placed an order for 30 in 1997, while major leasing company ILFC purchased 40, with a repeat order for a further 31. The only other airline to have bought the -600 is Tunisair, who ordered four in October 1997. The first -600 was rolled out at Renton on 8 December 1997, and it went on to complete its maiden flight on 22 January 1998. As of 31 January 1998, 122 -600s have been ordered.

Turning to the series 700, this version is similar in size to the -300, with a capacity to carry 128 passengers in a two-class cabin, or 149 in an all-economy fit. Since launch customer Southwest placed an order for 63 aircraft, with options on a further 63, orders have rolled in at a steady pace – Southwest alone has increased its requirement to an amazing 129 aircraft. Denmark's Maersk Air ordered six, followed a few months later

RIGHT *The prototype -600 (N7376) flew for the first time on 22 January 1998. This chunky aircraft, with its short fuselage and tall fin, appears somewhat out of proportion, but is easily identifiable when compared to other models. The aircraft is seen on the runway at Boeing Field at the end of a test flight.*

ABOVE *The European JAA finally recommended certification of the Next Generation series of 737s on 19 February 1998. This will permit Germania and Maersk Air to receive their first batch of aircraft, albeit some five months late. The aircraft illustrated here is D-AGEM, the second 737-75B for Germania, and it wears the colours of German tour company TUI. It was photographed departing on a test flight from Boeing Field on 9 February 1998 wearing the test registration N3502P*

by identical quantities for Germania and Bavaria Fluggesellschaft. The latter is now solely a leasing company, having terminated its airline operations some years ago, and two aircraft are destined for Transaero, the independent Russian airline. Elsewhere in Europe, established 737 operators Braathens SAFE and TEA Switzerland have both chosen the type to supplement/replace their new generation examples.

Although enjoying strong sales in Europe, the -700 has struggled to make an impact with US operators, although Continental committed to 26 -700s as part of an order for all three Next Generation models. A modest purchase of two aircraft came from Eastwind Airlines in October 1997, which will replace two elderly -200s currently in operation on the east coast, while Alaska Airlines ordered three aircraft the following month. In South America, Argentinian carrier LAPA will take two from ILFC, with another dozen slated to follow. Asian operator Shanghai Airlines has three on order, as has Air Pacific of Fiji. Given the popularity of the 737, further orders from China are likely, and during a visit to the USA at the end of October 1997, the Chinese President announced an order for a further 22 'baby Boeings', which are destined for employment with a number of 737 operators. Despite this success, Boeing will have to keep a weather eye on great rivals Airbus as the European consortium is at last making inroads into the 737's traditional market with its A320 family of jetliners.

Returning to a market not exploited since the T-43 of the early 1970s, Boeing has sold two Next Generation 737s to

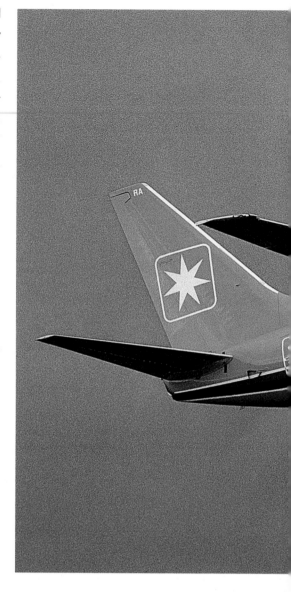

the US Navy, who has asked for these aircraft to incorporate a forward cargo door. Internally, they will be fitted out in the QC (Quick Change) configuration and will replace 29 venerable C-9B Skytrain IIs (militarised DC-9s) that have been in service since the early 1970s. Repeat orders for up to 20 aircraft are expected.

Boeing, in a joint venture with General Electric, has also modified the -700 airframe into a business jet aimed at the corporate market. Known as the BBJ, the aircraft will have the wing and landing gear of the larger and heavier -800, and be

available in a variety of interior cabin fits – no doubt a number will ultimately be operated by governments and heads of state. The aircraft will have a transatlantic capability, and Boeing has already received a number of orders.

The first Next Generation 737 was rolled out on 8 December 1996, this aircraft being a 700 series machine – it was also the 2843rd 737 to be built at Renton. Taking to the skies for the first time on 9 February 1997, the aircraft quickly completed its exhaustive flight test programme and first deliveries to Southwest and Maersk Air should have been made in October 1997. However, minor certification problems have come to light which have delayed their arrival in fleet service.

Firstly, the European Authorities required improvements to the overwing exits prior to certification, then, during flight testing, unexpected vibration was experienced on the horizontal tailplane. These problems were eventually overcome, and following FAA certification, the first -700 was delivered to Southwest Airlines on 17 December 1997. Rather than simply 'rub-

*By February 1998 Maersk Air had two -7L9s awaiting delivery. The first of these is OY-MRA, seen here with test registration N35153 climbing out of Boeing Field into a heavy overcast. The airline initially intends to use the -700s exclusively on charter flights*

BOEING 737-800

**ABOVE** *The prototype 737-800 (N737BX) taxies clear of the runway at Boeing Field after a test flight. This is the largest 737 variant built to date, and will remain so until the first -900 is constructed. The tail logos of the customers who have ordered this variant have been applied beneath the aircraft's window line*

ber stamping' the FAA approval, the European JAA took a little longer to satisfy themselves that these problems had indeed been overcome, and recommendations for certification approval were finally received on 19 February 1998. By 31 January 1998, -700 orders totalled an impressive 375, of which four had been delivered – all to Southwest.

When the Next Generation family was announced, the -800 was the largest of the trio of jets, being 3.02 m (9 ft 11 in) longer than the -400, and boasting a capacity of up to 160 passengers in a

mixed layout, and 189 in high density configuration.

Sales for the -800 have grown at a staggering rate since undisclosed orders for the first 40 jets were announced at the 1994 Farnborough Air Show. It was later revealed that German charter operators Air Berlin and Hapag Lloyd were the airlines involved, and since then it has been European operators which have proven most enthusiastic about Boeing's latest model. Amongst those who have selected the type are Air Europa, KLM, Lauda Air, LOT, Olympic, Pegasus, Sabre, Sterling

be their sole supplier of aircraft for many years to come. This deal included American's 'purchase rights' to acquire a further 425 737s! This was then followed by similar deals with Delta Airlines, who ordered 70 -800s and Continental Airlines who signed up for 30, although the latter figure has since been revised to 22 aircraft. Needless to say, Airbus Industrie was far from happy at such deals, and after protests from the European Union, the wording on the contracts was changed – although this is unlikely to change the deals in any way.

Elsewhere, China Airlines has six aircraft on order, while Jet Airways of India will also be an early recipient of the -800. In Africa the sole customer to date is Royal Air Maroc, who have nine on order.

The first -800 was rolled out on 30 June 1997 and performed its maiden flight on 31 July – first recipient of this variant will be Hapag Lloyd. By 31 January 1998, orders had been placed for 304 -800s.

The latest Next Generation variant is the -900, which was only announced on 10 November 1997 following receipt of an order for ten aircraft from Alaska Airlines, who have also taken an option on ten more. The airline plans to operate this variant in a two-class, 174-seat, configuration. Although Boeing had previously talked about the possibility of this variant, the unexpected launch with only one customer came as something of a surprise, and is certainly contrary to normal Boeing practice. This is the longest 737 yet, with a fuselage length of 42.1 m (138 ft 2 in) – just 5.22 m (17 ft 1 in) less than the 757-200! With development of the 757-300 well advanced, this could well signal the end for the 757-200.

European, Transavia and THY. The latter is the most recent customer, having ordered 26 examples, and placed options on a further 23.

Despite the number of European operators who have ordered this variant, numerically it is American companies who dominate. The order for 75 aircraft by American Airlines stirred up considerable controversy when it was revealed that this was part of a massive purchase which had allegedly been secured by Boeing through offering the airline preferential rates on the understanding that it would

# Boeing 727-200ADV

| | |
|---|---|
| 1 | Radome |
| 2 | Radar dish |
| 3 | Radar scanner mounting |
| 4 | Pressure bulkhead |
| 5 | Windscreen panels |
| 6 | Instrument panel shroud |
| 7 | Back of instrument panel |
| 8 | Rudder pedals |
| 9 | Radar transmitter and receiver |
| 10 | Pitot tube |
| 11 | Cockpit floor control ducting |
| 12 | Control column |
| 13 | Pilot's seat |
| 14 | Cockpit eyebrow windows |
| 15 | Co-pilot's seat |
| 16 | Engineer's control panel |
| 17 | Flight engineer's seat |
| 18 | Cockpit door |
| 19 | Observer's seat |
| 20 | Nosewheel bay |
| 21 | Nosewheel doors |
| 22 | Twin nosewheels |
| 23 | Retractable airstairs (optional) |
| 24 | Handrail |
| 25 | Escape chute pack |
| 26 | Front entry door |
| 27 | Front toilet |
| 28 | Galley |
| 29 | Starboard galley service door |
| 30 | Cabin bulkhead |
| 31 | Closet |
| 32 | Window frame panel |
| 33 | Radio and electronics bay |
| 34 | First class passenger cabin, 18 seats in mixed layout |
| 35 | Cabin roof construction |
| 36 | Seat rails |
| 37 | Cabin floor beams |
| 38 | Cargo door |
| 39 | Anti-collision light |
| 40 | Air conditioning supply ducting |
| 41 | Forward cargo hold |
| 42 | Cargo hold floor |
| 43 | Baggage pallet container |

| | |
|---|---|
| 44 | Tourist class passenger cabin, 119 seats in mixed layout |
| 45 | Communications antenna |
| 46 | Fuselage frame and stringer construction |
| 47 | Cabin window frame panels |
| 48 | Air conditioning system intake |
| 49 | Air conditioning plant |
| 50 | Overhead air ducting |
| 51 | Main fuselage frames |
| 52 | Escape hatches, port and starboard |
| 53 | Wing centre section No.2 fuel tank |
| 54 | Centre section stringer construction |
| 55 | Cabin floor construction |
| 56 | Starboard wing No.3 fuel tank |
| 57 | Inboard Krueger flaps |
| 58 | Krueger flap hydraulic jack |
| 59 | Leading edge fence |
| 60 | Outboard leading edge slat segments |
| 61 | Slat hydraulic jacks |
| 62 | Fuel vent surge tank |
| 63 | Navigation lights |
| 64 | Starboard wing tip |
| 65 | Fuel jettison pipe |
| 66 | Static dischargers |
| 67 | Outboard, low speed, aileron |
| 68 | Aileron balance tab |
| 69 | Outboard spoilers |
| 70 | Outboard slotted flap |
| 71 | Flap screw jack mechanism |
| 72 | Inboard, high speed, aileron |
| 73 | Trim tab |
| 74 | Inboard spoilers |
| 75 | Inboard slotted flap |
| 76 | Fuselage centre section construction |
| 77 | Pressurised floor over starboard main undercarriage bay |
| 78 | Auxiliary power unit (APU) |
| 79 | Port main undercarriage bay |

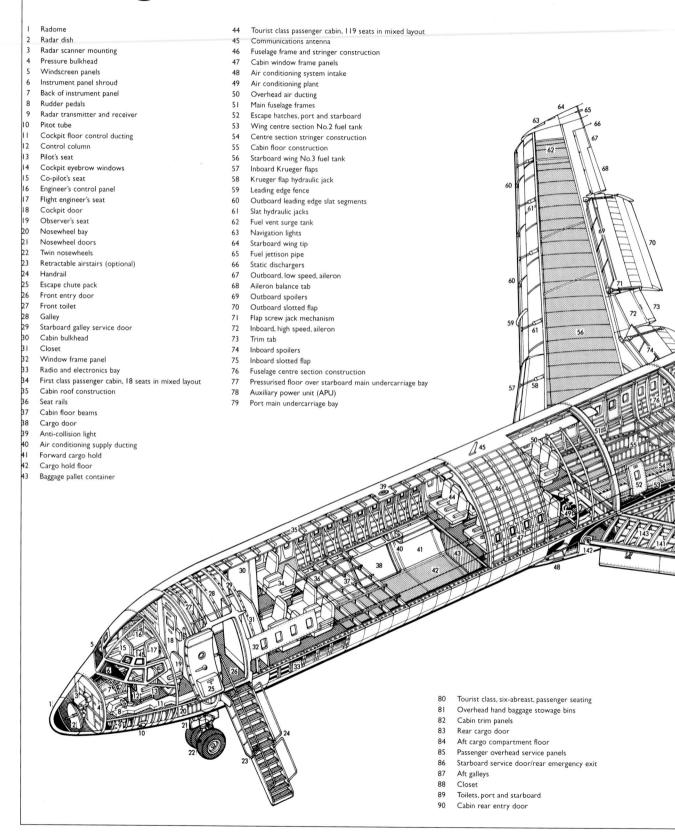

| | |
|---|---|
| 80 | Tourist class, six-abreast, passenger seating |
| 81 | Overhead hand baggage stowage bins |
| 82 | Cabin trim panels |
| 83 | Rear cargo door |
| 84 | Aft cargo compartment floor |
| 85 | Passenger overhead service panels |
| 86 | Starboard service door/rear emergency exit |
| 87 | Aft galleys |
| 88 | Closet |
| 89 | Toilets, port and starboard |
| 90 | Cabin rear entry door |

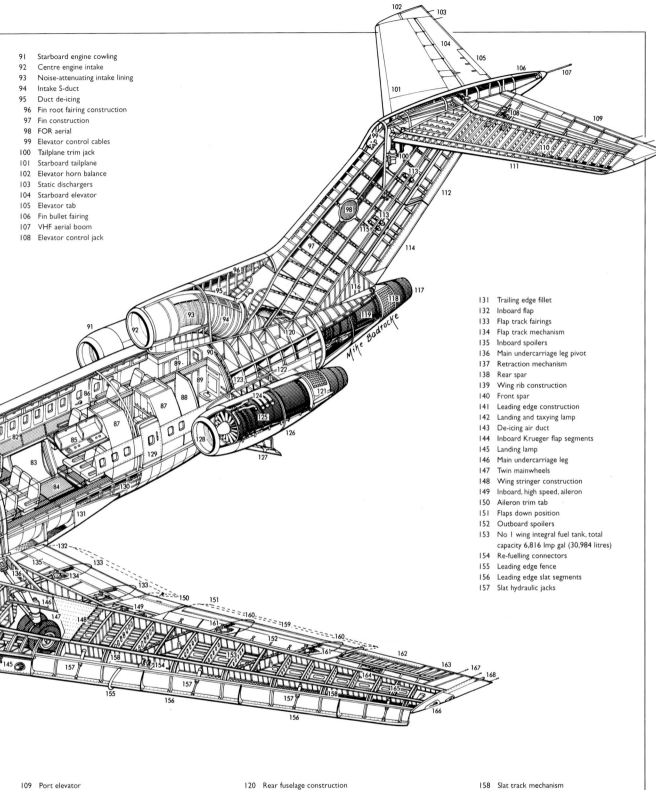

91  Starboard engine cowling
92  Centre engine intake
93  Noise-attenuating intake lining
94  Intake S-duct
95  Duct de-icing
96  Fin root fairing construction
97  Fin construction
98  FOR aerial
99  Elevator control cables
100  Tailplane trim jack
101  Starboard tailplane
102  Elevator horn balance
103  Static dischargers
104  Starboard elevator
105  Elevator tab
106  Fin bullet fairing
107  VHF aerial boom
108  Elevator control jack

131  Trailing edge fillet
132  Inboard flap
133  Flap track fairings
134  Flap track mechanism
135  Inboard spoilers
136  Main undercarriage leg pivot
137  Retraction mechanism
138  Rear spar
139  Wing rib construction
140  Front spar
141  Leading edge construction
142  Landing and taxying lamp
143  De-icing air duct
144  Inboard Krueger flap segments
145  Landing lamp
146  Main undercarriage leg
147  Twin mainwheels
148  Wing stringer construction
149  Inboard, high speed, aileron
150  Aileron trim tab
151  Flaps down position
152  Outboard spoilers
153  No 1 wing integral fuel tank, total
     capacity 6,816 Imp gal (30,984 litres)
154  Re-fuelling connectors
155  Leading edge fence
156  Leading edge slat segments
157  Slat hydraulic jacks

109  Port elevator
110  Tailplane construction
111  Port tailplane
112  Rudder upper section
113  Rudder control jacks
114  Rudder lower section
115  Lower section trim jack
116  Centre engine mounting pylon
117  Centre engine exhaust pipe
118  Thrust reverser
119  Centre engine

120  Rear fuselage construction
121  Slide engine thrust reverser
122  Engine pylon fairing
123  Rear pressure bulkhead
124  Bleed air system pipes
125  Pratt & Whitney JT8D-9A turbofan engine
126  Detachable cowlings
127  Rear entry ventral airstairs
128  Engine air intake
129  Port rear service door/emergency exit
130  Lower lobe fuselage frame construction

158  Slat track mechanism
159  Outboard slotted trailing edge flap
160  Flap track fairings
161  Outboard flap track mechanism
162  Aileron balance tab
163  Outboard, low speed, aileron
164  Aileron control jack
165  Fuel vent surge tank
166  Port navigation lights
167  Static dischargers
168  Fuel jettison pipe

# Appendices

## Appendix A
### Specifications

### 727-100

| | |
|---|---|
| First flight date: | 9 February 1963 |
| Maximum accommodation: | 131 |
| Wing span: | 32.92 m (108 ft) |
| Length: | 40.94 m (134 ft 4 in) |
| Height: | 10.36 m (34 ft) |
| Maximum take-off weight: | 76,692 kg (169,000 lb) |
| Range at maximum take-off weight: | 3218 km (1738 nm) |
| Cruising speed: | Mach 0.78 |
| Maximum ceiling: | 36,000 ft |

### 727-200

| | |
|---|---|
| First flight date: | 27 July 1967 |
| Maximum accommodation: | 189 |
| Wing span: | 32.92 m (108 ft) |
| Length: | 46.69 m (153 ft 2 in) |
| Height: | 10.36 m (34 ft) |
| Maximum take-off weight: | 95,027 kg (209,500 lb) |
| Range at maximum take-off weight: | 4635 km (2500 nm) |
| Cruising speed: | Mach 0.74 |
| Maximum ceiling: | 37,000 ft |

### 737-100

| | |
|---|---|
| First flight date: | 9 April 1967 |
| Maximum accommodation: | 115 |
| Wing span: | 28.35 m (93 ft) |
| Length: | 28.66 m (94 ft) |
| Height: | 11.28 m (37 ft) |
| Maximum take-off weight: | 50,350 kg (111,000 lb) |
| Range at maximum take-off weight: | 2945 km (1590 nm) |
| Cruising Speed: | Mach 0.73 |
| Maximum ceiling: | 37,000 ft |

### 737-200

| | |
|---|---|
| First flight date: | 8 August 1967 |
| Maximum accommodation: | 130 |
| Wing span: | 28.35m (93 ft) |
| Length: | 30.48 m (100 ft 0 in) |
| Height: | 11.28 m (37 ft) |
| Maximum take-off weight: | 58,105 kg (128,100 lb) |
| Range at maximum take-off weight: | 4179 km (2255 nm) |
| Cruising speed: | Mach 0.73 |
| Maximum ceiling: | 37,000 ft |

### 737-300

| | |
|---|---|
| First flight date: | 24 February 1984 |
| Maximum accommodation: | 149 |
| Wing span: | 28.88 m (94 ft 9 in) |
| Length: | 33.4 m (109 ft 7 in) |
| Height: | 11.13 m (36 ft 6 in) |
| Maximum take-off weight: | 62,822 kg (138,500 lb) |
| Range at maximum take-off weight: | 4204 km (2270 nm) |
| Cruising speed: | Mach 0.745 |
| Maximum ceiling: | 37,000 ft |

### 737-400

| | |
|---|---|
| First flight date: | 19 February 1988 |
| Maximum accommodation: | 170 |
| Wing span: | 28.88m (94 ft 9 in) |
| Length: | 36.45 m (119 ft 7 in) |
| Height: | 11.13 m (36 ft 6 in) |
| Maximum take-off weight: | 68,040 kg (150,000 lb) |
| Range at maximum take-off weight: | 3870 km (2090 nm) |
| Cruising speed: | Mach 0.745 |
| Maximum ceiling: | 37,000 ft |

### 737-500

| | |
|---|---|
| First flight date: | 30 June 1989 |
| Maximum accommodation: | 132 |
| Wing span: | 28.88 m (94 ft 9 in) |
| Length: | 31.0 m (101 ft 9 in) |
| Height: | 11.13 m (36 ft 6 in) |
| Maximum take-off weight: | 60,550 kg (133,500 lb) |
| Range at maximum take-off weight: | 4481 km (2420 nm) |
| Cruising speed: | Mach 0.745 |
| Maximum ceiling: | 37,000 ft |

### 737-600

| | |
|---|---|
| First flight date: | 22 January 1998 |
| Maximum accommodation: | 132 |
| Wing span: | 34.31 m (112 ft 7 in) |
| Length: | 31.24 m (102 ft 6 in) |
| Height: | 12.6 (41 ft 3 in) |
| Maximum take-off weight: | 65,574 kg (144,500 lb) |
| Range at maximum take-off weight: | 5981 km (3717 nm) |
| Cruising speed: | Mach 0.782 |
| Maximum ceiling: | 41,000 ft |

### 737-700

| | |
|---|---|
| First flight date: | 9 February 1997 |
| Maximum accommodation: | 149 |
| Wing span: | 34.31 m (112 ft 7 in) |
| Length: | 33.63 m (110 ft 4 in) |
| Height: | 12.56 m (41 ft 2 in) |
| Maximum take-off weight: | 69,885 kg (154,000 lb) |
| Range at maximum take-off weight: | 6009 km (3245 nm) |
| Cruising speed: | Mach 0.781 |
| Maximum ceiling: | 41,000 ft |

### 737-800

| | |
|---|---|
| First flight date: | 31 July 1997 |
| Maximum accommodation: | 189 |
| Wing span: | 34.31 m (112 ft 7 in) |
| Length: | 39.47 m (129 ft 6 in) |
| Height: | 12.56 m (41 ft 2 in) |
| Maximum take-off weight: | 78,244 kg (172,500 lb) |
| Range at maximum take-off weight: | 5246 km (2930 nm) |
| Cruising speed: | Mach 0.785 |
| Maximum ceiling: | 41,000 ft |

### Notes

- For all new and next generation variants, the maximum speed is Mach 0.82.
- Insufficient data has yet been published to include the 737-900 here. It will, however, be 42.11 m (138 ft 2 in) long, and have the same wing span as the rest of the Next Generation family.

## Appendix B
### Production and Delivery Information (as at 31 January 1998)

| | Number Ordered | Number Delivered |
|---|---|---|
| B727-100 | 572 | 572 |
| B727-200 | 1260 | 1260 |
| **Total B727s built** | **1832** | **1832** |
| B737-100 | 30 | 30 |
| B737-200 | 1114 | 1114 |
| B737-300 | 1122 | 1037 |
| B737-400 | 481 | 445 |
| B737-500 | 383 | 356 |
| B737-600 | 122 | 0 |
| B737-700 | 375 | 4 |
| B737-800 | 304 | 0 |
| B737-900 | 10 | 0 |
| **Total B737s built** | **3941** | **2986** |